The
HOle
Truth

J. B. LIPPINCOTT COMPANY
Philadelphia and New York

The HOle Truth

INSIDE BIG-TIME, BIG-MONEY GOLF

Tommy Bolt
with Jimmy Mann

BOLT, Thunder, Lightning,
National Open Winner...
        but He Prefers TOMMY.

LATE one wintry afternoon more than forty years ago, two young boys, dressed far too scantily against the descending cold, were stealing themselves some holes of golf.

Stealing is the word for it, for in those days in Shreveport, Louisiana, it was mostly the rich, male adults who played golf. Some of the rich, male adults had young sons. It was seldom any of these youngsters were seen on the golf course. Never, to be sure, in the kind of weather Shreveport was having this day.

The Broadmore Country Club was Shreveport's best. There were three holes cut back in a wooded area far from the clubhouse, far from the protective eyes of any of the club's custodians. It was on these three holes that Tommy Bolt and his friend had sneaked to play and to freeze this afternoon.

"I can't play anymore," said the friend. "I'm turning blue. I have to go home."

7

"You can't quit," said Tommy. "I've parred the first two holes. Let's play this one more. I gotta see what I can do."

There was water in the fairway of this third hole that Tommy Bolt was so anxious to play. The huge lake reached out from the right into the fairway. The golfer had to play close to the water in order to have a reasonable second shot to the green. Par for the hole was four.

Tommy raced to the tee, struck his drive perfectly at the right-hand corner of the water. The ball hooked slightly, bounded on the fairway, and tossed and rolled some 200 yards to a perfect position.

His friend sliced his tee shot. The ball hit the fairway short of the water but kept bounding fiercely The last the two boys saw of it, it disappeared below a giant spray in the lake.

"Damn it," said the friend. "I'm through now. That was the last ball I had. I'm not freezing to death. I'm going home."

"Wait," said Bolt. "Wait, I'll see if I can get it for you. You have to play this hole with me. I want to see if I can par these three holes. I'll get your ball for you."

Bolt raced to the lake's edge. Without hesitation, without giving the numbing weather a thought, he kicked off his shoes, peeled off his socks, rolled his pants knee high, and waded into the lake. It was but seconds before his toes located a ball on the bottom. He stooped, lifted it and tossed it to the bank. "Here, hit it!"

Reluctantly, the friend pulled a three-wood from the single bag of clubs the two boys were sharing and struck the ball toward the green.

Bolt bounded to his shot. As he approached, he pulled an iron club, letting the rest of the clubs fall to the earth. He stood over his ball only a second, then turned his shoulders and sent a zooming shot ringing off into nightfall.

As the boys drew near the green they saw that Tommy's shot was no more than two feet from the cup. Still barefooted, Tommy leaped with joy. The cold was nothing to him. The excellence of that single shot warmed him as much as the potbellied stove he had waiting for him at home. He picked out the community putter, raced to the flag, pulled it, dropped it on the green and then leaned over his putt. He struck it and the ball rolled perfectly into the cup.

"A birdie!" screamed the ecstatic Bolt. "My fi⁻st birdie! And it was my first round of golf under par."

Yes, to Tommy Bolt in those days, three holes was a round of golf.

Some twenty minutes later, as the two shivering youngsters turned a corner, soon to part to claim their own doorsteps, Bolt turned to his friend. "Don't ever say you're going to quit out there. We are lucky we don't get caught. We must do most of our playing on days like today. When it is cold like this no one will ever catch us. That birdie should teach you that we must never quit as long as there is a place to play and we are able to swing at the ball."

His embarrassed friend nodded and replied through chattering teeth, "It's the worst fun I've ever had. If the weather stays this cold, they'd have to pay me to get me back out there."

Tommy, running for home, yelled over his shoulder, "Someday they just might be paying you."

Just a few months ago, Tommy, now fifty-three, was aboard a 707 jet liner en route from his plush home in Sarasota, Florida, to the West Coast, where he was to spend the week playing golf at a ritzy country club with the opportunity to win a lot of money.

"We had been in the air some time," Tommy remembered. "Why, I don't know, but I just happened to look out of the window. It was a clear day and you could see the ground.

"And there it was. There was the Red River, the big river that divides Oklahoma and Texas. I stared at it a long, long time and then I relaxed deep in my seat, closed my eyes, and thought a lot of things. A whole lot of things."

Tommy's reflections aloud ended. But it was easy to trace his thoughts on this particular day.

It was in Haworth, Oklahoma, on March 31, 1918, that

9

Tommy was born. His mother died when he was an infant. His father, Walker Bolt, seeking a better life for his three children, two sons and a daughter, loaded them in a covered wagon and crossed the Red River into Texas. The family stayed there only a short time and then traveled to Shreveport, Louisiana, where Tommy went to school. And it was during his early school days that he and his brother, J. B., became regular members of the caddie corps at the Lakeside Country Club.

Tommy doesn't remember his score the day he played his first eighteen holes of golf. He remembers only that he was twelve or thirteen years old. He also recalls that it was not very long before he was playing well, well enough to "get hooked enough to play in freezing weather."

Today, golf is played by young boys and girls all over the country. In forty years golf has spread from the pastime of the idle rich to the masses. Today the cost of golf is far lower than it was during the years when Tommy Bolt used it as a means to earn pocket money. His caddying days at Lakeside gave him a glimpse of the lure of golf. His dream of becoming a star was far from a reality.

It was after he had quit high school and left his family that he became a sincere devotee of the game. This was made possible with wages he earned as a carpenter. He had joined a construction team contracted to build army bases throughout Texas. "I must have helped build five or six of them" Tommy remembers. "And in each town we worked I'd find the nearest golf course. Whenever we were through working, I'd grab my bag of fourteen little friends and go looking for the action."

Tommy was near twenty now. During his years he had done three things. He had swung someone else's golf bag from his shoulder as he caddied for half a buck a day. He had swung a hammer with his construction team and found the work profitable but painfully unexciting. And he had swung his own golf clubs This excited him. He could not get it out of his mind. It was freedom. It seemed to him that golf offered him the only means to escape the hammer, nails, and time clock.

"The first time I gave golf a serious thought," he says, "was in Abilene. The cats fell out of the woodwork there. When I got time off from my job I'd find them standing around with money jammed in all pockets. Cash without a home, boy!

"And there were tournaments almost every week. I had never been able to play in any tournaments because of my work. These things were so tempting. I put the hammer in mothballs and stuck close to my little 'fat' friends and those amateur tournaments."

If the rules covering amateurism in golf had been as stringent in those days as they are today, then history would record that Tommy Bolt was turned professional by the United States Golf Association in the late 1930s in Abilene, Texas.

"That's a fact," he agrees.

Tournament officials aren't allowed to give amateur golfers money as a prize. The reward is usually merchandise, a set of irons or woods. Or a golf bag. Or many golf balls.

Tommy would win these tournaments and sell his prizes. "I would go to the tournament," he recalled. "They would always have the prizes displayed. I would see what they were offering and then spend the early part of the week finding me a buyer. I always managed to find me a fellow who promised to take the prize off my hands for cash. Then I would have me something to shoot for."

And what happened when there wasn't a golf tournament?

"Well," Tommy explains, "I had me a little dentist and a lawyer who just loved to play during the week. They'd bet their money and we'd go at it almost every afternoon. I guess during those days those two fellows set a world record for getting beat one up. They nearly won every time, but Old Dad would make something happen so he got the casheroo."

That "something" is old hat. By that time Tommy had gained full control of his golf swing. Not only had he managed to acquire a winning golf swing, but he had managed to acquire one he could control. One, as today's golf pros describe it, that holds up when the heat is on. Meaning simply, the greater the pressure, the better the swing.

As all good things must, Tommy's good days at Abilene came to an end. They ended when Uncle Sam wrapped Tommy Bolt in khaki for a 3½-year obligation in the Corps of Army Engineers. They put him there because when he was inducted he told them he had been a carpenter. But later, as almost all servicemen do when they survive the initial shock of induction, he wised up and found a more tolerant ear. Into this ear he whispered that he hadn't always been a carpenter; he had also been a very good golfer. The result was that Tommy ended up in Rome, Italy, with the Army's Special Services division. He was golf professional at one of Rome's elite golf clubs which had been converted to an American officers' club by occupation forces.

"This was a very exclusive club," said Bolt. "But Mussolini was antigolf. Two of the club's eighteen holes had run along Via Napoli. Mussolini hadn't wanted the traveling public to see his people playing golf so he had those two holes plowed under. He made a sixteen-hole course out of it, hidden by woods."

Bolt's years in service did nothing to take away his undying desire to play golf. In fact, these years did much to improve his game, and he is well aware of his good fortune at being stationed at the Italian golf club.

But it was not this period that determined him to become a golf professional. Had that been the case, his trip home might have been a bit more calm.

"We came home from England," he recalled, "on a boat with some guys we heard were prisoners of war. At first, we thought they were Americans who had been captured by the enemy and released. We found that this wasn't the case. They were Americans okay, but they were nasty cats. They were Americans who had been imprisoned by the U.S. Army in England.

"I had a pretty good bundle of cash with me when I left England. Had I been convinced I was good enough to play the golf tour, that money would have come in handy. I would have had enough to at least try it. But I wasn't thinking about the tour. I was planning to return to Shreveport and go to work for my dad on a construction job. Thus, when the card and dice games started on the boat, I was right in the middle of them.

"It turned out the prisoners had spent the war learning all there was to know about rolling dice. They free-rolled those things."

Tommy didn't like the way they were rolling the dice, but he, like the rest of the "straight" soldiers in the game, wasn't inclined to say anything. It would have been a long swim.

"Those guys seemed to group together," he said. "We knew their backgrounds and we were content to lose just our money. I guess everybody on the boat lost something, but we never questioned the honesty of the game. It's the old story, if you don't think it's fair, why play?

"If you ask that question, then you've never been on one of those troopships coming home from war.

"I went busted somewhere out in the middle of the Atlantic and it didn't bother me. I knew I had work waiting for me when I got home."

Construction work around Shreveport was going well after the war, and Walker Bolt welcomed his son back with plenty of work and a brand-new hammer. But Tommy had not forgotten his golf and wasn't inclined to permit loyalty to his father to come between an afternoon with the suckers on the golf course.

"I played every Saturday and Sunday legally," said Tommy. "But Monday was a work day and Monday was also a day that a lot of guys gathered at the course for a little action. Every Monday, I would work until noon and then they'd have to hunt me. I was gone."

Not more than a year later, Tommy was finding himself following the same footsteps he had walked just before the war in

13

Abilene, Texas. He was winning nearly all the amateur tournaments in the Shreveport area on weekends and cleaning the pockets of his "little mullet" on the weekdays.

"This was the period I was choosing between construction work and professional golf in my mind. It had marked the second time I figured those mullet were easier to kill than those nails were to hit. But as an amateur, a man has to find a lot of people who want to gamble and he has to beat nearly all of them to make ends meet."

Tommy thought he had made his final break from the construction gang in late 1946 when a group of friends from Tallulah, Louisiana, suggested that he turn professional and offered him $1,000 as an incentive to try the PGA tour.

Tommy found this attractive and agreed. "I went to Fort Worth and missed the money by a couple of shots. Then I went to Montgomery, Alabama, and won a hundred and seventy dollars. It was the first money I'd ever won as a pro and my second tournament. I remember that I stayed at the YMCA in Montgomery. Then there was golf at Atlanta, Orlando, Tucson, Phoenix, and San Antonio.

"I made money in a few of them," he remembered. "But not enough. Atlanta was where I first knew that I could play pro golf with those guys. I was paired with Lew Worsham at the Druid Hills Country Club. He was good, good enough to win the tournament. But I came away from there feeling that he was not that much better than I could be.

"The thousand dollars, plus what I won along the way, lasted for eight tournaments. But the cash soon got away from me and I was back in Shreveport. Back with that hammer and looking for work."

Someone told him that Houston was growing. There was plenty of high-paying construction work in Houston. In 1947, Tommy went there as a carpenter.

"Man, the hardest thing I ever did was to nail those boards together in Houston during 1947, 1948 and 1949 when they were

14

playing the Houston Open. I never went near the golf course while the tournament was going on. I couldn't have taken it.

"When I first went to town, I played at Herman Park. Then I heard there was a lot of action around Memorial Park. I took my little cash out there and battled those hustlers for three years. What it amounted to, honestly, was hustlers trying to kill a pretty good hustler."

It can be recorded that Houston, Texas, was the site of the last nail Tommy Bolt ever drove for money. He was there only a couple of years when he finally quit construction work for good. He hadn't struck it rich, but he had found himself enough pro-amateur tournaments and enough mullet to make it while he worked endlessly at perfecting a game that would work on the professional tour.

"It was sometime during this period that Howie Johnson (now a star on the PGA tour) moved to Houston. He and Dave Marr (a former PGA champion) used to win prizes in amateur tournaments and bring them to me.

"They had shotguns, golf clubs, outboard motors, everything you can imagine. I'd put up cash against them and play their best ball. I ended up with the prizes. Dave used to caddie for me regularly in those days, too."

Among the Houstonians Tommy golfed with regularly was a well-known and affluent hair-growing specialist named Sid Mueller. Sid was a loser, of course, but he admired Tommy very much. Near Christmas time of 1949, Sid gave Tommy $800, no strings attached, and urged him to try his hand in the Miami Open. Tommy took it. Jim Ferrier won at Miami, but Tommy Bolt finished third. Tommy collected $750. The next week, a handpicked list of pros was invited to participate in Havana. Jimmy Demaret got Bolt's name on this list. He did not finish high in Havana, but all the players made some money and the trip was worthwhile.

Tommy's next visit to Houston was brief. He spent most of his time playing his final rounds of golf there and telling his friends

15

good-bye. His hammer was gone forever. In early January of 1950 the PGA tour was starting in Los Angeles and among the new faces that year would be an ex-caddie from Shreveport, Louisiana, Tommy Bolt.

"There I was," he recalled, "a tournament player."

"Oh, those cold mornings when we also-rans would have to break the ice in the ball washers and go about our business getting out of the way of the big stars of the time. I played all the way around to Miami. And I didn't play well. I kept thinking that next week would be it. And I guess I kept thinking that if next week wasn't it, then there was always that hammer."

His frustrations peaked in the spring in Miami. He led the golf tournament, but shot 42 on the final nine holes and earned only $220. Jacksonville lay ahead and then Greensboro. His pockets were nearly empty. After his disappointment in Miami, he did what very few golfers in the history of the game have ever done. He sold his golf clubs for $100 so that he could get to the next tournament.

"I didn't give it a thought that I was going to a tournament without golf clubs. My only thought was I'd have to have cash to meet the entry fee, the lodging, the food, the caddie expenses.

"At Jacksonville, I got me a set of clubs out of the back of Bob Watson's car. They were good ones and I made another two hundred dollars."

Though he hadn't made much of a dent on the tour and was nearly busted again, Tommy had impressed officials of the Kroydon Golf Company, Maplewood, New Jersey. Shortly after the Jacksonville tournament, he was signed by Kroydon for very little money, but with the assurance he would be supplied with golf clubs. "That was my only thought. I needed sticks."

He made his way to Greensboro, played the tournament, but Sunday afternoon found him with just enough money to clear his debts.

A friend, Ed Tipton, told him that a professional at nearby Chapel Hill, North Carolina, was looking for an assistant. Bolt

16

told himself that it was time to go back to steady work. Golf was his choice, for he had vowed he had driven his last nail.

It was in the week that followed that what seemed to be the worst thing that could have happened to Tommy occurred, although, as it turned out, it was the very best thing that ever happened to him. He frequently looks back on the seeming disaster with humor that is hard to understand unless you understand Bolt.

His 1941 Nash automobile had given signs during its swing from California to Florida and then to North Carolina that it was tired and sought permanent retirement. But Tommy, stopping frequently along the road, kept the machine moving with waste oil.

"I was just a few miles out of Chapel Hill and away from my new job when the car stopped," he recalls.

"I called a friend of mine in that area for money. He didn't send money, but he told me of a man in Durham, North Carolina, who owned a driving range and wanted a professional to run it for him.

"I still was interested in the job in Chapel Hill, but first I wanted my car fixed. I called my sister and she sent me a hundred dollars. It took sixty-five dollars to fix the car. There were no guarantees. The rest was spent for lodging and food while the mechanics worked a week."

During that week, Tommy inquired about the assistant pro job in Chapel Hill. He found it paid very little, not even enough to allow him the slightest savings. When his car was ready, he called Leamon Couch, the man with the driving range in Durham. When he and Bolt completed their telephone conversation, Couch had a professional for his driving range. The 1941 Nash made its final trip of twelve miles.

"I stayed in Durham about one year," Bolt said. "Leamon Couch is a true friend of mine. He did many things for me during that year. One of the first things he did was help me get another car. I traded that '41 Nash for a 1948 Chevrolet Bel Air. This is important to the story, for eight months later, I crawled into that Bel Air and took off once more for the tour."

During the year Tommy stayed at Couch's driving range, he played considerable golf around Durham—always looking for those mullet who might serve as his means to continue his play on the tour.

But the life of the driving range operator is a confining one. The name Tommy Bolt was meaningless to the natives, although word had gotten around that he had played the PGA tour for a while. This encouraged a number of people to request lessons at the driving range.

"I worked hard at those early lessons," Bolt said. "I felt that with the lessons, and my pay, I would be able to save some would begin giving them in the afternoon some days and go right up until midnight. I have always said that this was the hardest work I have ever done in my life."

During the summer of 1951, Bolt had saved a few dollars. Couch gave him the Chevrolet and a $100 bonus and Tommy drove to Detroit. "I played well there, but I was under considerable pressure. I had been in that rat race twice before and each time was forced to retreat. I probably didn't say ten words to any of those cats in Detroit. I was there to play golf and that's all I did."

He finished in the money, but not high. He won $150. Three weeks later, he played in the St. Paul Open. He won $750.

"I think that was it," he said. "Mark this down as the starting point for me. I wasn't rich in money. In fact, there had been times in my life when I owned more money than I did after that St. Paul tournament. But I had something far more than money. I had the knowledge of what it was like not playing the tour—driving nails and running a driving range. I knew the only life for me was the tour. It caused me to protect my money and work harder than ever on my golf."

Tommy played a few more tournaments, but nothing exciting happened to him. To the best of his recollection, he broke about even in winnings and expenses.

In those early days, the concluding PGA event of the year was the annual North and South Open at Pinehurst. Bolt arrived back in Durham, visiting his friend Leamon Couch, a couple of weeks before the Pinehurst event.

"I had played that Pinehurst Number Two course many times," he said. "Long before the tournament was to be played, I felt that I would do well. The course is long and narrow in some places. A man can't go on it with just a good putter and expect to beat a group of golf professionals. Pinehurst Number Two demands good golf, not merely good putting."

When the smoke cleared the weekend of the North and South Open in Pinehurst in 1951, Tommy Bolt had won his first PGA tournament. Tommy still lists this among his top thrills as a professional golfer. And there is good reason. In 1951, the Ryder Cup matches were played at Pinehurst prior to the North and South tournament. In Ryder Cup competition, all outstanding British and American professionals gather for four days of competition. Bolt, naturally not an American Ryder Cup player that year, was the longest of long shots to wipe out such a lusty field.

If the money Tommy won during the summer at Detroit and St. Paul was the fuel which jetted him toward stardom as a touring professional, then his win at Pinehurst was certainly the second stage. His final orbiting came just two months later when he tacked on the first prize in the Los Angeles Open. It was the opening tournament of the 1952 season.

"Sweet as a peach," he recalled. "We played at the Riviera Country Club. That was the big club out there in those days. All those movie stars were seated up on that hill overlooking the eighteenth green as we played our final rounds. I remember I tied Dutch Harrison and Jack Burke. We had to playoff on Monday.

"Bing Crosby followed us during the playoff. I was tickled to death he thought enough of golf to walk eighteen holes with us. Since then, however, I have found out how much he loves the game. He has been a friend of golf for many years."

Despite victory in the first tournament of 1952, Tommy did not crash the select top ten in money winnings that year. But he was in the top fifteen and confident that he had arrived as one of the stars of the game.

Few people cared to hear just how Tommy Bolt had gotten to this point of stardom; the fact was he was there. The players regarded him as an outstanding player, one who refused to be bullied and one who refused to shirk the work required to make a champion. The PGA officials did not take him in as a pet in those early days and have done little since to indicate that they realize he has ever meant anything to golf at all. The fans, however, loved him. They loved to see him throw clubs. They loved to see him hit great shots. He was a gallery favorite for one reason or another. He realized this and gave them what they wanted, good throws and good golf.

He quickly adapted to tour life. He made the top ten money winners in 1953, 1954, and 1955. His one brief low point came in May of 1955. He had begun hooking the ball fiercely. Whereas in past years he was able to protect against this dollar-wasting plague that has seized all manner of golfers over the years, it was 1955 when he decided to do something permanent to eliminate it entirely from his game.

"Right after the Colonial Invitational in Fort Worth, I asked Ben Hogan to help me get rid of that hook," said Tommy.

"Ben proved to be a true friend of mine. He did it. A thousand times since he helped me I have made it public that I thought he was the greatest friend a man could have. And each time I give him the credit, he lets me know that he appreciates it. He has ways of letting you know those things."

It was with the advice that Hogan gave him that he won the bulk of his sixteen PGA victories. And it was with that swing that he won the 1958 National Open Championship, the ultimate thrill of his career.

But somehow, Tommy Bolt has passed through golf without

20

the recognition he really should have. His earnings in golf, well above the $300,000 mark, have him trailing only Sam Snead from that immediate post-World War II era. It makes one ask, What about Byron Nelson, Lloyd Mangrum, Dutch Harrison, Craig Wood, Gene Sarazen, Jim Ferrier, Jack Burke, Jimmy Demaret, Ted Kroll, Cary Middlecoff, and the rest? They are there, but they trail Tommy Bolt at this point.

"I don't like to think in these terms," he says. "But it is true that I have passed many of the great players. But that really doesn't matter. It gripes me that they look at Palmer's money winnings and say that he is the greatest golfer of all time. Goodness, what if Sam Snead had received the purses Palmer received? Case closed."

Bolt admirers everywhere have been wondering when in the world the PGA was going to get around to the rubber stamp procedure of placing Tommy's name in the golf Hall of Fame?

What does a player have to do? How long does he have to be a great name in the sport? Who could have done more to promote the game? Few people will ever know how many C-notes Tommy has laid on players who have come upon hard times or even caddies who need the money to get to the next tournament. Tommy has been the softest touch on tour for twenty-five years.

Of course, you don't make golf's Hall of Fame giving away $100 bills. But what about his third-place finish in the 1971 PGA Championship? He provided the drama for a tournament Jack Nicklaus was about to do away with. Not bad for fifty-two years of age, huh?

Though he was in his prime just a few years before television brought the giant purses to golf, Tommy has entered a period in which senior golf is growing to fantastic proportions.

There are two big senior professional tournaments each year, one sponsored by the PGA, which he has won once in three tries, and another—the National Senior Championship—which he has won three consecutive times.

He and Sam Snead are considered the most durable golf players who ever lived. Bolt concedes that Snead who is fifty-eight, is remarkable for his age. But he is not surprised.

"Those young kids out there would like to know they are going to be as durable as Snead," he says. "Why, his tempo is so great that he will be hitting great golf shots when some of those stars out there now may be buying tickets to watch him play."

Bolt, too, has acquired a tempo that makes his swing effortless. It puts little strain on his body, and he has few of the aches and pains that plague even the younger players on tour.

At fifty-three, he is still a star in his profession. Throw out Palmer and Jack Nicklaus, and Bolt has more national television commercial time than any other golfer in the world. He works for Faberge and its subsidiary, the Tone-O-Matic Company. He still goes at his profession as diligently as a man half his age. He has never ridden a golf cart eighteen holes in his life. He is a walker and refuses to play unless he can walk.

There is nothing complex about Tommy Bolt. He does what he feels has to be done. He says what he feels has to be said. He knows that at times he may trample toes. But he never tramples toes unless he brings along ten of his own to be trampled. He stands willing to accept the consequences.

You will read later that he tells mothers they should keep their sons at home. "Don't let them play professional golf," he says. "It is not a good life for them. I have a son of my own and I'd much rather see him be a doctor or lawyer. The game has been good to me, but not all the people who run the game. Some have been bad to me and bad for golf."

He has a legion of friends among all the great players of golf, not the least of whom is Ben Hogan, perhaps his closest friend. What grieves him most is to hear players (not Hogan, incidentally), whisper their grievances against the PGA but not have the courage to complain in the open. Never one to whisper himself, Tommy grows impatient with those who whisper to him. It is beyond his imagination why the men who made golf with their skills are so afraid to speak openly if their feelings would do the sport justice. He says what he thinks.

Why does Tommy Bolt, who is far from a bitter man, say these things? Why, all of a sudden, does he come along and appear as an authority on all things connected with golf? Well, there's a very good reason.

Bolt is unique in golf's passing parade. Although he was there right after the war when it all started, he is not a has-been. He made two false starts at the profession, then a third and successful one. This is evidence he knows all the highs and lows of the profession.

He becomes indignant when he reads or hears of the PGA doing what he terms an injustice to the likes of Hogan or Snead or himself. He thinks it was ridiculous that the PGA insisted that a "rule is a rule" and that Hogan was forced to tee off at 7:27 A.M. at Westchester, New York, in the summer of 1970. He says that the PGA considers the pioneers of the organization the officials who never missed a payday in their lives, not the struggling players who put up their own cash to provide the show. The odd part about it all is that Bolt has smacked them repeatedly with the truth. "It had always been dog-eat-dog out there," he says. "But today it is callous, commercial to a fault."

There is indication that perhaps Tommy didn't spend all his time on the practice tee when he was just beginning to appear on the PGA tour. He obviously spent much of his time listening to other players talk. For after twenty-five years he has come away knowing an awful lot about what went on when he first started and what is going on now. And in a historic straightforward style, he has given answers to all the questions.

First, however, when was he forming all these opinions?

There was a four-year period after the war when Tommy alternately tried the professional tour and retired back to construction work. A good part of the Bolt of today was molded in those years. This was the first time he experienced the typical frustrations of professional golf. He was a nobody, and that alone

23

rubs fiercely against the Bolt grain. He always went far out of his way to make friends. His fault was probably attempting to make everybody like him. He took for granted those who did and rejected and rebelled against those who did not.

On this subject, he has said, "I always wanted everybody to like me. I wanted the guys I played with to like me, and the fans. It was a long time before I found out this was impossible." Even today this has been a hard reality for Tommy to accept.

It was impossible for him to hide the fact that he did not like someone. If a player had shown Tommy an unfavorable side, then Tommy did not want to play golf with him. Time and again he chastised the pairing committee for putting him with certain players. But this was a cut-and-dried rule of golf. There was nothing that could be done. Tommy had to live with it and there were times when he was unable to.

The fact that Tommy could not understand personality clashes, the reason that some players acted indifferent and hostile toward him, was one of the things that delayed his climb to a perch of high regard among the country's leading tournament players. Indeed, this blooming professional star is a sensitive, temperamental man who refused to understand that there should be any outside aggravations for the athlete attempting to perfect a winning golf swing. He has always campaigned on the plank that the tournament player should be free of any worry other than making the exact golf swing that the moment demanded.

Any outside interference enraged him. He was quick to degrade another player who intruded on his concentration. He would attempt to correct a spectator whose deportment was unbecoming to the seriousness of the game. But he reserved a generous part of his wrath for the officials of the game, the PGA officials. He could not understand how these high-salaried people who took the players' money and gave them little in return could and would enforce such stringent rules on a large company of human beings who, after all, had the all but impossible assignment of becoming one of the ten best golf players in the world.

Yes, in Tommy's first years on tour, you made the top ten or you merely broke even or lost money for the year. Few players ever took to professional golf back in those days unless they figured that someday they would be the best in the country.

"Yes," Tommy agrees, "I did get angry. But I was not the only man out there getting angry. I admit I was quick to show it. I let it come now!

"But there were others, many, many others. The list of frustrated golfers I've played with and seen is much longer than the list of great players. I do say one other thing. I left my wrath on the golf course. You never heard of me carrying it back to the motel and taking it out on my wife."

This, it can be supposed, was an honorable trait. But sports writers covering golf tournaments, and Tommy Bolt's part therein, weren't so understanding. Few, if any, of them ever reported that "Tommy Bolt got it all out of his system today at the thirteenth hole when he hooked his tee shot. Bolt then cursed violently at a spectator, threw his club, and stalked resolutely to the clubhouse. Some twenty minutes later, Bolt was on the practice tee. He was his old self once more. He had a few drinks at the bar with friends, wished them all well, and drove away in good spirits toward the tournament a week from now."

The writers chose to relate just Tommy's actions on the course. That was good enough for them. The reason for it or the result later mattered little to them. It did, however, matter to Bolt.

It was early in his career when he finally decided that golf was not a game that a man would be permitted to play freely. He saw early that there would be outside distractions, and he armed himself against them. He wasn't one of those locker-room whisperers who found fault with many things but refused to do anything about it other than whisper to other players. When it went against the Bolt grain, he went straight to the man in charge. He yelled loud and long. He took it on as his personal fight.

"And there were many times," he said, "when they figured they did me a favor listening. When I left, another official would come around and ask, 'What was that crybaby in here about this time?'"

He had one characteristic that at least made them listen. Tommy made sure that every time he went to anybody with a gripe he had truth on his side. "I could tell early that the truth hurt them," he said. "But still they didn't do anything about it simply because they had been running things their way all those years. They resented anybody trying to change it, especially someone who charged them like a bull."

Bolt has always armed himself with the truth. It was blunt, sometimes cruel, and always harsh, but it was the truth. He corrected everybody—the press, the players, the officials, and the ticket-buying fans, everybody. Those who were targets of the Bolt venom were far outnumbered by those who became his friends. He also captured those who, though not his close friends, admired him for either his hell-bent attitude toward getting wrongs corrected or his undying dedication to perfecting his golf swing, or both.

Tommy combined temper with a quick wit, a midwestern drawl, and a distinct knack for coining phrases or nicknaming things and people. He was never vicious with his argot. Rather, he distinguishes himself with it. He has passed through tens of thousands of locker rooms in his time, spent decades with golfers, thinking golf and talking golf. Nearly everything Tommy Bolt does or thinks pertains to golf.

Nothing about golf is sacred to Tommy. Nor is anyone connected with the game safe from his wit, which often is as subtle as barbed wire. He just loves to get in the middle of a golf argument with a platoon of Arnie's Army. Most of the people on Palmer's side knew the great star only after he became the king of the fairways. Bolt and Palmer go back to 1955, the year Palmer began as a struggling tour player.

"I'll tell you how well I know him," says Bolt. "In one of his books he wrote that I helped him win the Canadian Open. He was leading the tournament and I was paired with him. On one of the late holes he hooked the ball deep into the woods. Yeah, the King has hooked one or two in his time.

"When I got down there, there he was, an iron in his hand, ready to knock the ball through the trees. He was desperate. I told him, 'Man, chip that thing back out there in the fairway. You are about to win this tournament. Don't try to knock it through those trees, you might make ten.'

"He did what I told him, but he didn't like it. Then he hit his third shot on the green, made his putt, and got his par. He won the tournament."

Bolt has never begrudged Palmer one ounce of the recognition he has gained through golf. But Bolt does become disgruntled when the idea is mentioned that Palmer made golf what it is today. It does dig into him a bit when it is suggested that Palmer is the greatest golf player who ever lived. Bolt firmly believes that golf did as much for Palmer as Palmer did for golf. He says it without flinching. And no one is going to convince him that Arnold Palmer could ever hit a golf ball with the knowledge and authority that Ben Hogan had in his prime.

"Not only does Hogan know more about hitting the golf ball than Palmer," says Bolt, "but he knows more about it than Palmer and the other four top players in the world."

His favorite dig at Palmer, and again this is friendly, just out loud, is when the discussion comes around to Bolt's victory in the National Open in 1958. "Where was Arnie?" he will ask. "Where was the Masters Champion that June in Tulsa?"

Well, Palmer was right there. But Bolt was sixteen shots ahead of him. Palmer, at 299, was tied for twenty-third position. Bolt won with 283, beating Gary Player by four shots.

Though always amused, the listener must be up on golf's argot to understand everything Tommy is telling you when he is discussing a particular hole he just played. He might say:

"The wind was humming in pretty good. Those other two cats I was playing with hit over there somewhere, far away from the pin. I looked a moment, snatched my little five-woodsky out of the sack and pop! . . . sent that little jessie right in there at the joint."

What he was saying is that he chose a five-wood from his bag and stroked his golf ball near the flagstick. He will not bore you with his delivery. He has too many variations. The ball, depending on his mood, might be "that little jessie," a "dimpled darlin'," a "white rat" or a "dart." He is definitely one of the "now" gang. You meet him now, you like him now.

In a recent pro-amateur, one of his partners whom he had never met before was an attorney, Art Beneditto. Bolt said nothing to the man during the first hole of play. In fact, the only thing he had ever said to the man in his life was, "How are you doing?" And that was at the first tee.

But Beneditto hit a violent hook off the second tee, a very tight hole. Bolt bellowed, "Hey, Maf, you put the Harley on that jessie. When things close in out there you got to cool that little jewel out on the fluffy."

Beneditto never did get the translation. What Bolt was saying, roughly, was this. He called the fellow "Maf," short for Mafia; he got that idea because the guy was a lawyer and was Italian. He hates to see any golfer try to guide the ball. It reminds him of someone attempting to drive a motorcycle through a narrow passage. Since Harley Davidson is the motorcycle he is most familiar with, he says, "You put the Harley on that jessie (ball)." "When things close in out there you got to cool that little jewel out on the fluffy," means simply when the fairway is tight, slow your tempo and the ball will fly straight to the close-cut fairway.

Asked later if he remembered the incident and thought the guy understood his message, Bolt answered, "I guess so. He strapped some law talk on me later. And I jurisprudenced him all over the place."

There has always been a pure faith in the hearts of the

American public. The feeling is that when mass America puts its stamp of approval on a man, be he a political figure, an entertainer or a dedicated professional athlete, then that man is rightfully deserving. The term has been, "the fickle public." Perhaps, it should be changed to "the selective public."

The public took a long, long time deciding about Tommy Bolt. "I know I kept them in a state of indecision," he said. "Back early in my career, I threw just a few golf clubs, and, yes I broke some, too. The public, with the aid of the press, was quick to label me 'Terrible-Tempered Tommy' and many other things. It got so that the public expected me to throw clubs and I obliged them.

"I launched far more because they expected me to than I did because I was mad at anything that had gone wrong with my golf. And, I never in my life threw anything but golf clubs. Why, I read that I once threw my caddie and then walked into the water to retrieve him. I've never even gone into the water to get a golf club. I've been in water once in my professional life and that was to hit a golf shot. That's the only time."

Strangely enough, Tommy has lost only one golf club in his life as a result of his temper—or his self-assigned obligation to his public. "Usually," he explains, "when I would throw a club toward water, I'd pick me a spot near the bank. I knew how far I could throw every club in the bag. So, when I threw toward water, I'd release it so that it would land near the bank on one side or the other. Then it would be easy for the caddie or some friendly spectator to retrieve for me.

"Back in the early 1950s, before there were many fans and when I was launching them after a bad shot and meaning it very much, I had me a little 'sucker' (or mullet, as Tommy refers to his gambling opponents back in the early tour days) down at the Bayshore Golf Club in Miami. We used to always try to get a little action going before the tournaments. Our goal was to make the week's expenses from these people and then whatever we won in the tournament was gravy.

29

"On this day, the lamb was killing the butcher. The mullet wasn't playing his role. He was playing well and I was having a heck of a time trying to keep my own cash in my pocket.

"On a very key hole in the match, I hooked my drive into a large lake. Man, I was hotter than a depot stove. I was using this very good Ben Hogan driver made by MacGregor. I think it was nicknamed 'the Bomber.' It was a great club. I might have parted with a finger or two, or at least three toes, before I would have this club. But at that moment, the veins sticking out an inch in my neck, I was intent on getting this dude airborne.

"Out there to the right of the tee, not more than twenty-five feet wide, was as harmless a canal as you have ever seen. I had no fear of getting the club far from either bank. I picked that target and tried to throw a skimmer, one that would hit in the middle of the canal and skip near the far bank.

"It was a bull's-eye. But something told me the moment the club disappeared under the water that I was in trouble. After you've seen a few of them sink, you can just about tell how deep the water is. This one didn't look right to me. I walked down there and the closer I got to the canal, the deeper it looked. Finally, I asked the caddie and he told me it was thirty or forty feet deep. Well, it turned out he was half right. It was seventy-five feet deep.

"That little incident cost me seventy-five dollars. After the round, I hired a diver to try to get it for me. He couldn't find it. I let him dive seventy-five dollars worth, paid him off, and called it quits.

"If there was a bright note to the day, I later turned the tables on that mullet we were trying to scale. I got his hand out of my right pocket, but the diver put his in my left pocket. Those were the days when a seventy-five dollar loss like that could take its toll on a guy's concentration in the golf tournament."

Bolt loves to reflect back to others he has seen throw golf clubs. "Why, during those early days Palmer was on tour, he threw them. I have to say that he was the very worst golf-club thrower I have ever seen. He had to learn to play well, he'd have never made it as a thrower.

"Winnie, Arnold's wife, was as good at retrieving them as I have ever seen. Arnie would put one of those duck hooks on a shot and then, without aiming at anything, let it go. He might throw it behind him. But Winnie was there. She'd pounce right on it. I know Arnie never lost one. At least, I know Arnie and Winnie never lost one.

"The PGA fined me once for throwing a club in jubilation. I hit a fine shot and the fans were howling and yelling and congratulating me. I tossed the club up in the air as sort of recognition of the applause. This cameraman, trying for some sort of Associated Press prize or something, started clicking away while my club was going up and coming down. Next day they had a picture in the paper of the club about four feet over my head. I was making an obvious attempt to catch it, but did that matter to the PGA? Not one bit. It cost me a hundred dollars.

"Twice within the past two years, I saw pictures in various papers of players throwing clubs. Once it was Tom Weiskopf, the other time it was Palmer. I clipped them out and mailed them to the officials. I attached a note, 'Okay, let's see that these guys get fined.' I never heard a word. You can bet they didn't."

Bolt admits there is little wonder that the public took plenty of time to finally appraise him. He has read the audits of hundreds of sportswriters throughout the country, most of whom say he has permitted his temper to cost him $500,000 in prize money. But today, he lives far better than any of the sportswriters who have taken it onto themselves to evaluate his temper against the success he might have known.

"It hasn't cost me that kind of money," he said. "In fact, my temper, that is the reputation I had for temper, and my ability to turn it off and on, has made me money through permanent recognition."

Just recently, many diligent members of the press have come to forget Tommy's temper and amplify his ability to strike a golf ball. Among the most cherished clippings he has stowed away in many thick scrapbooks are ones written of the days he has hit eighteen consecutive greens, had his approach shots riding straight toward the flagstick on each occasion. The determining factor of the round was how many feet he was long or short of the hole.

"Earlier," he said, "I played rounds with Hogan when he was doing just that. Oh, the monotony of the thing. It seemed to me that he would be the only man alive to ever hit a golf ball that straight."

Perhaps it was the players themselves who really got the temper tag off Tommy's back. For in many instances in recent years when outstanding players on tour were asked who they considered to be the best striker of the golf ball in the world today, many of them immediately voted for Thomas Henry Bolt.

Tommy is an athlete, his physical coordination defying all the supposed inroads of age. He is perhaps as good an athlete today as he ever was. That alone would make Bolt the best-preserved athlete in the history of American sport.

The counter to this might be: "Bolt is not the winner on the PGA tour he used to be. How in the world could anyone imagine he is playing as well or better than he ever played in his life?"

The rebuttal: "The tour isn't as easy as it used to be. Bolt has played professional golf for twenty-five years. He won less money in those early years, but he won more often.

"Yet, today he and Sam Snead are recognized as the two best senior golfers in the world, a senior golfer being a player who has passed his fiftieth birthday. But Bolt is not satisfied with the total life of a senior and from time to time takes his amazing talent to war with the day's young lions of the PGA tour.

"The scores Bolt returns today are as low as they were when he was a youngster on tour. It is just that there are more and better players in the competitions. But today Tommy is scoring as well as he ever did. And that's amazing, and testimony for his theory, 'My health is my wealth.'"

32

Try the association test.

What does the name Tommy Bolt mean to you?

Are you a member of the clenched-teeth brigade? Do you see Tommy clenching his teeth, raring back and throwing his driver or putter as far as he can throw it? Do you remember him red-faced, filled to the eyeballs with rage? Was he walking off a golf course in complete despair the last time you saw him? Was he quitting in the middle of a round? He did these things, you know. He has quit a golf tournament when all he had to do was walk six or seven more holes and collect big money.

Or, did you once caddie for Bolt? And did Bolt find fault with you and fire you? It wasn't all your fault. Nor was it all his fault. He is, putting it as plainly as possible, a spirited competitor. A man who combines outstanding talent with fierce dedication and competitiveness. No one associated with him, not a wife, not a son, not a business partner, not even a caddie can be anything less.

To fail, to Tommy Bolt, is to die a little. He said, "If you die a little many times, sooner or later you will die for good. That doesn't interest me."

You could not be blamed if you said you remembered Bolt more for temper than for talent. But, oh, the thousands who recall this name just because they have seen him at work.

Maybe they were along that week in Tulsa in 1958 when he was crowned the National Open Champion. This is the biggest golf tournament of them all. Tommy won it after he had passed his fortieth birthday.

"I had the secret that week," he said. "I was happy. Happy all over. Nothing could have made me mad. I knew the minute I hit the first shot I was the winner. I was the complete master of my emotions. This is so important to a golfer, to a person. To everyone. It is important to be able to apply yourself totally to what you are trying to do. That week in Tulsa, I did it perfectly."

But it wasn't the first hole at the Southern Hills Country Club in Tulsa that won the National Open Championship for Tommy

33

Bolt. It was the twelfth hole, a 445-yard, slightly dog-legged par four.

For four rounds, the best field of golfers that could be assembled charged into that twelfth hole and fell back thoroughly defeated. Sand, trees, and water were their undoing. All week long the scoreboard attendant was busy writing fives, sixes, and sevens in those small boxes running down from the number twelve hole at the top of the sheet. But none were found by Tommy's name. That week he played Southern Hills' twelfth hole, three-three-four-three, three under par, an awesome display of superiority.

This is how many remember Tommy Bolt. They remember they saw golf played as only he could play it during the high points of his long career.

There are still others who remember Tommy. They don't even recall that he is or has been known throughout most of his career as a man of violent temper. They know he is one of the game's outstanding players, but, yet, there is something else they remember better. Tommy Bolt did something for them.

Say you know someone Tommy Bolt has hurt? Then there is a man over here who knows a hundred people Tommy Bolt has helped. Tommy is not a man who wants credit for anything. He is a man who once or twice needed help, got it, and in return has helped as many others as he possibly could.

"Among the good things the Lord has done for me," Tommy said, "is at one time in my life He permitted me the privilege of being poor. The privilege of honestly needing people and of feeling the joy of receiving their friendship. It has meant much to me. It certainly makes it hard for me to turn down the fellow who comes along with that sincere need."

And they come. Young golfers come to Bolt for help. They have put their lives in golf, and their swings are so confused through trial and error that they have sought out this man as their last resort.

"I feel, and I certainly hope they do, that each one of them left

34

me knowing more about their trade. It was my goal to set them on the right track. That was all I could do. The rest depended on their dedication to their chosen profession."

Bolt often tells of the time in 1955 when he needed help with his golf swing. He went to the best player of the time, Ben Hogan. Hogan put Bolt on the right road. It was Bolt's effort, as Hogan advised at the time, that assured the success of the lesson. Bolt worked hard at what Ben told him.

It should be understood now that nearly all the people who have had any interest in golf for twenty-five years will know Tommy Bolt one way or another. They may remember temperament, talent, or beneficence. But the point is that Bolt has been seen by thousands of people during his golfing career and hardly any of the witnesses ever forgot the man.

Will he go down as one of the country's millionaire athletes? Nope, he won't make that plateau. But he'll have many of the things a man strives all his life for. He'll have comfort, luxurious comfort. He'll have the thing he worked on for forty years, his majestic golf swing. He'll have his legion of true friends, not the least of whom is Ben Hogan. And he'll live in the satisfaction of knowing that though he was not a teen-ager with long hair, not a hippie, he too raised his voice in protest. And, unlike many other protestors, Tommy Bolt did not do the screaming until he had waged the war personally and won. He was on top when he tried to reach back and help.

When you boil it down tight, Tommy said most of it forty years ago on that cold night in Shreveport:

"Don't ever say you are going to quit out there!"

The HOle Truth

*How do you compare the golfing breed with athletes
in other sports?*

Physically, the football, baseball, basketball, and ice hockey
players certainly should have the best of it. They are involved in
running games. There is physical contact, punishment. But
mentally, including competitiveness, self-discipline, determination, there is no contest. The winning golf player is far superior to
the star player in any other sport.

You must remember, athletes in other sports merely have to
perform to receive their pay. Golfers must win to get paid. Can a
game be any tougher, when you have to gamble your sole income
on your skill?

How many professional football players would there be if the
officials said: "You pay us to play quarterback. When you win the
Super Bowl, we will then give you a hundred thousand dollars"?

How many baseball pitchers would there be if they were told: "Pay us a hundred dollars a game. If you win the pennant, then we will pay you fifty thousand. If you then win the World Series, you get another fifty thousand"?

There wouldn't be any professional football and baseball under those conditions, I'll assure you. But that's the way it is in golf. In fact, it is tougher than that in golf. They don't say here is a $150,000 tournament, go show us what you can do. They make the young players of today pass through a rigid, approved players' program. This is an elimination round before the candidate even gets off the ground, but it is the only way it could have been worked out. And when the young player of today passes that first test and receives his players' card he has actually nothing more than a license to prove his competitiveness, his determination, and his sheer guts. He has nothing more than a card which entitles him to report to the tournament each Monday and attempt to qualify for the big tournament which begins on Thursday. And there are so many young men there on Monday shooting their hearts out for the few spots open to them on Thursday.

But what does this success guarantee the young man? Absolutely nothing. He must shoot a very good score during the first two rounds of the tournament to qualify for the final two days—Saturday and Sunday. And what if he does that? Well, he'd better play his career golf for two days or he has finished far down the list and his week's work has cost him money, for the prize at the bottom of the list does not cover a week's expenses these days.

The answer is simple. A player can succeed, so to speak, at golf and starve himself right off tour. The answer is that he must win or he must finish very high each week—say the top twenty-five or thirty. There is none of the minimum salary business for the rookie golf player, that you find in the rest of the sports.

I would like to point out, however, that it has not always been so sweet in football, baseball, and basketball, either. I'll give players like Stan Musial, Ted Williams, Joe DiMaggio, and some of the great who rose before these high salaries and bonuses all the credit. I know they made their way to the top of the heap with non-livable salaries when they first started—but nevertheless they were getting paid to play. They weren't spending their own money each time they put on that uniform.

No doubt about it. It takes far more competitive heart to rise to the top in golf than it does in other sports. Far more.

Golf isn't without personalities from other sports. Along the way we've had athletes come over to our profession after they had succeeded at another. Sammy Byrd played the tour twenty years after playing the outfield for the New York Yankees. And it is history that Sam never did anything in golf to compare with his playing the outfield in Yankee Stadium. Ellsworth Vines was a champion tennis player who tried the golf tour. More people remember Elly Vines, the tennis champ, than Elly Vines, the golf champ. John Brodie, quarterback for the San Francisco 49'ers, tried the pro golf tour. Know where he is now, don't you? Think John wouldn't rather be picking up a nice $7,000 golf check each Sunday afternoon instead of wondering when one of those 300-pound defensive tackles is going to puncture one of his lungs?

And there's another out there today. Jesse Whittenton, the all-pro defensive back for the Green Bay Packers, is giving golf a try. Who would you think had more determination in sports than a smallish defensive back for a pro football team? Well, the answer is simple: a guy trying to make his way on the professional golf tour. He'd better have more heart, for he is out there all alone and if he errors, there's no free safety man to come over and help out. Wonder if Jesse has ever hit a bad shot on tour and just for an instant hoped that maybe a teammate would be there to cover his error? That probably was the lonesomest day in Jesse's life, the day he found out he was now a tour golfer and that it is not a team sport.

Did you ever hear of an athlete in another sport having his pay cut off because he was in a slump? No! They arrange for the guy to take additional practice. They work with him. What happens to the slumping golf player? Well, he spends more of his own money. Might as well be throwing it in a creek. And just hopes that he pulls out of his slump before he pulls out that last $50 for the entry fee. This race is sometimes very close. Sometimes the golfer loses the race, other times he wins it. But it seems this is always one determined by a photo at the wire.

There's no one to pull the golf professional out of his slump but himself. Years ago, when a tour player was swinging poorly, there were certain guys out there who deliberately told him wrong things to push him farther downhill. The feeling was the more guys you sent home, the better off everybody would be. That doesn't work today. Send one guy home and there's a good chance some kid will pop out of that rabbit pen and win everything everybody has.

Professional golf can probably be termed the world's biggest legalized crap game. It is nothing but an outright gamble. You have to have a certain amount of "hustle" in your blood or you wouldn't take the chance they require you to take. You wouldn't put up your money with no guarantee of any return if there wasn't some gambling blood coursing your veins.

Probably a super ego goes right along with this superior fighting heart the tour player owns. The newcomers on tour today are mostly college graduates. They could go into many other fields. But they feel that they have what it takes to become winners on the tour. You'd think they would be blinded by the glamour surrounding Palmer, Nicklaus, Casper, and the rest of the big ones. They are not. They know there is glamour, but only after hard work. And they have that super ego that keeps them working toward the day they can bask in the glory of the game. The hardest workers will make it.

Athletes from all other sports have used their minds along with their skills and dedication to obtain livable salaries for today and, more importantly, excellent pensions for tomorrow. But not the professional golfer. Oh, lately some of these young lions, these toothless young lions, have shoved the parent organization, the Professional Golfers Association of America, a trifle. There has been pushing. There have been threats. There has been a bluff or two. But what has it gotten the players? Salaries? Pensions? Nothing.

Golfers, I repeat, may not be as physically endowed as the tarzanians of other sports. But golfers possess far more determination. They have a tremendously high threshold of self-denial. And guts! The lowest pro golfer of the top sixty each year is probably as gutsy as the fiercest pro football player. I honestly believe that. I say it because that golfer, to make his way to Number Sixty in the world, had to do it alone. He was his own franchise. It was do or die with him and him alone. Did that fierce pro football player make himself stand on that football field day after day, week after week, month after month, practicing, practicing, practicing? No. He was regimented into it. He was paid to do it. The golfer chose to gamble with his talents, his time, and his cash. That took guts. The professional golfer, I mean the tour player, is a breed of cat who chose to go it alone. The association he joined doesn't pay him a salary. This is something which adds to the many pressures he already endures during the tournaments.

Are most of the touring professionals looking for some lucrative country club job during their travels around the country?

Nooooooo, sir.

When you read of a well-known touring professional quitting the tour and taking up residence behind some pro-shop counter then you know he has done it as a last resort. I say this from experience. In 1957, I quit touring and took a job at the

43

Knollwood Country Club in Los Angeles. I signed with them for a year and it was like being in jail. I couldn't wait until that year was up. They couldn't either, mind you. They said I was playing too much golf.

I did play a lot of golf. But that is my business. I gave them a nice, well-stocked pro shop. I thought I was there enough. But I wasn't happy at all. And when the contract ran out it was like someone had lifted the fog off London for me. I felt as if I had been paroled.

There's a joy in having some fifteen-handicap golfer at one of those tournaments point you out and say, "There's Tommy Bolt." It's a lot better than being tied to that pro-shop counter and having that same fifteen-handicapper storming in and saying, "Where's Tommy Bolt?"

You find many home professionals telling themselves that they are perfectly happy where they are. That they wouldn't swap what they are doing for anything in the world. They are kidding themselves. There are very few, very, very few home pros who at one time or another didn't dream of themselves waltzing down that eighteenth fairway at the Doral Country Club needing only a par four on that final hole for the championship. They didn't have the competitive heart or enough determination to fight for it, and therefore they ended up nursemaiding 400 or so members who can be outrageous in their demands on a golf professional.

There's a lot of excitement, thrill, glory, satisfaction, and fulfillment hitting one of those $1.25 balls on tour. But there's absolutely none when you have resigned yourself to selling them to eighty shooters for a living. In my opinion, a fellow who has tasted success on tour never would make a good home professional. As soon as he begins that daily routine he starts getting itchy feet. He picks up the paper, reads about the tournaments, and every week he sees a chance that he might be making $1,000 or so.

I know how it is. None of them are too much different from me. I got real lucky, however. The year after I left Knollwood, I won the National Open in Tulsa. And as I look back on it, I feel that the year I took off and practiced and played a lot rested me and got me ready to win the Open. But another thing, when I left I knew I was through with that home professional life for good. Knew that it would be the tour or nothing. I was in the proper frame of mind. The indecision was gone. Here I was, back on the tour. And if it didn't work, I was out of golf.

For a couple of years there, Bobby Nichols, a fine player and one of my favorite people, didn't do too well on tour and took a pro job at the Firestone Country Club in Akron. This settling down enabled Bobby to be with his family more, something that he needed. But it had to hurt him. Bobby was just thirty-four years old, and a wonderful player. It wasn't long before he was back out there. And it wasn't long before he was winning. He won the rich Dow Jones Championship and that $60,000 first prize. During the Dow Jones you could see that Bobby was going to be the winner all the way. No one was going to rush that swing. He had perfect control of himself. His swing was slow, compact, and dedicated as if to prove that surely this was not a home professional winning, but a solid touring professional performing exactly where he was supposed to be.

Bobby has had a good career as a touring pro. I remember back in the early 1960s when he first came on tour. I liked him then. In fact, I gave him the first two pairs of Foot Joy golf shoes he ever owned.

So many times good touring pros go into a decline and begin trying to analyze the reason. Many times they figure that they are missing their families. Their children are growing up fast and they aren't spending the time with them they feel they should. This certainly takes away some of the concentration they should be applying to their golf. Then they look for and find a reasonably good pro job. But soon they're relaxed again, hitting the ball simply great and raring to get back out there. They owe something to their club. They feel that they owe something to themselves. Here they are really torn between loyalties. But really, down deep, it is no contest. They know they would rather be out there running that rat race each week.

It's really something to see these tour players deal with the clubs when the time comes for them to leave the tour. I don't think one of them signs with a club without some provision in the contract saying he can play so many tournaments a year. Right there he is making it plain to me that he isn't convinced he is going to be exiled forever to that pro-shop counter. It's not long before that little six-by-twelve space becomes a jail cell. Friend, I've been in one of them.

What's with these golf pros that need it so quiet to perform?

Don't blame us, blame "the Good Man" who made us as we are.

I know, they cheer and boo at baseball games, at football games, at basketball games, at ice hockey games, and sometimes at tennis matches. So, who do we golfers think we are?

They told me about the fellow who attended his first golf tournament with a friend. They stationed themselves behind the ninth green and hadn't been there forty minutes before the first-timer whispered to his companion. "Last time I had to be this quiet was at a funeral."

First, let me say that we (nearly all golf professionals, and nearly all golfers) have some mysterious immunity to site noises. For instance, if the golf course is located near an airport, the sound of one of those 747s burning cash and rubber to escape the ground doesn't bother us in the least. We shield that noise. Even if a hole is cut near an expressway, we can make good swings and putts in spite of engine noise, screeching tires and horn blowing.

It is simply a case of knowing the condition exists. Somehow, I'm not sure how, we can prepare for that type of noise.

But, if an airplane is taking off half a mile away and ten feet away someone is whispering to his neighbor, the whispering could distract us no end. If a golf professional missed the shot, he wouldn't go looking for the airplane pilot, but he might think of parting the hair of that whispering fan with a five-iron.

Golf is a game of little action and a lot of concentration. Good golf is a game of total concentration. Any sudden noise can break that concentration, bring about a flinch and send that ball into water, out of bounds or into a jungle. In golf, unlike baseball, we have to play the foul balls.

Still, it is not always the fault of the fan. When a golfer is having trouble concentrating, he's experiencing a bad day, he is looking for something to lay the blame to. I've seen them so edgy that they complained when a lady powdered her nose—the noise of that powder puff on that pretty nose got to them.

Back in the days when every other fan in the gallery used to carry a camera, Sam Snead and Mike Souchak did everything but arm themselves with hand grenades. Oh, did those two hate the sight of those things. If it were Sam's turn to hit and he spied someone with a camera, he'd warn them not to use it. If they slipped up on him and annoyed him with it just once, he'd yell, "Get out of here with that camera."

It never bothered me to see people with cameras—it bothered me when I didn't see them. I wanted them to want to take pictures of me. In my opinion it was an excuse when Snead and Souchak complained about cameras. They weren't concentrating as they should have. I guess I recognized this because the same thing, in a different way, has happened to me.

At Tulsa in July 1971, during the PGA Championship, Tony Jacklin, Mike Hill and myself came to the tee of a short, easy, par four hole. I wasn't playing well. My concentration was horrible.

Just as we reached the tee, I saw these small boys, maybe eight

47

to ten years old, playing by a pond just off the tee. The minute I saw them, I knew they were going to interfere with my shot. Imagine thinking that badly. I know Hill and Jacklin saw them, too. But they never gave the kids a second thought. But me, good old Tommy, I had to find me an excuse and there they were, two little boys, and I was ready to lay the crime to them. A crime, mind you, that hadn't been committed.

Both Jacklin and Hill smacked tee shots straight and true. My turn. Sure enough, I hit an awful shot. Just as I reached the top of my swing, one of the boys said something to the other. It wasn't all that loud, but had he just turned his head, I would have used that as an excuse. My concentration was gone.

Maybe it was because they were so young, maybe because I couldn't locate a marshal or maybe because I'm older and a bit more passive, but I didn't say a thing to them. I simply stared hard their way and walked to my ball.

When the hole was done, I had a six. I scratched around and made double bogey, one hateful extra stroke for each of those little boys. It was this hole that led to me having the back trouble which subsequently caused me to withdraw from the championship. Oh no, I didn't hurt the back swinging, the back started hurting when I dropped that little putt for the six. Don't let them fool you, lifting heavy objects, kidney trouble, nervous tension isn't the primary cause of back trouble. Nothing will give a touring professional back trouble quicker than double bogeys. You can withdraw without penalty with an ailment. And a sore back is a sure-fire free ticket home to many golf pros. Check it out sometime, the fellow who quit last week with the sore back is that same fellow who finished third this week. Where'd he get that miracle cure? Why doesn't he sell it to the medical world?

Here's some more about noise and concentration and good shots and bad.

I was playing a practice round once with some amateurs. We were midway through the front nine and preparing to hit our approach shots to the green. Off to the left, a member of the maintenance crew was busily cutting the rough. His tractor was chugging along and he was pulling a couple of gang mowers. Three of us hit to the green and all the shots were well placed—good ones despite the noise we had blocked out.

Just as the fourth player reached the top of his swing, the maintenance worker cut off the tractor's engine. You should have seen the result of that. The shot was hideously shanked.

You see right there that noise and concentration are connected. The rumbling of that mower hadn't bothered three players and it wouldn't have bothered the fourth, but the moment it stopped, it was doomsday for that swing. Had the player been concentrating on his golf swing, rather than blocking out that noise, he would have done well. The key here is to concentrate on the single thing you can control, swinging that golf club, not something outside that you have no control over.

They tell this story on Patty Berg. Once this fine veteran woman professional had a key shot on the final hole of a tournament. Just as she addressed her ball, the shrill whistle of a passing train cut through the late-afternoon stillness. Patty completed her swing and sent the ball dead straight at the green, ten feet from the hole. She won the tournament with it. Later, someone congratulated her: "Patty, that was an amazing golf shot. We're glad that train didn't bother you." Patty answered, "What train?"

That afternoon Patty Berg had had complete control of herself. This is the important thing with all the championship golfers of all time.

Sure, the game grew under the "Hospital Zone" atmosphere. All golfers have made their swings on lonesome practice ranges where there was little or no noise. And there never was much sudden noise. All golf professionals look back to those tireless hours of practicing alone—themselves, their clubs, and their practice balls. You learn to play in those surroundings and I guess that's the way you grow to expect it when you graduate to tournament competition.

49

Someone should hold a golf tournament someday called the "Nerve-Tester Open." Fans should be armed with whistles, firecrackers, movie cameras, all types of noisemakers. Make it a real anything-goes affair. My bet is that the same guys winning now will win under those conditions. The guys who concentrate on their business the best will win in a forest fire.

Why is it that when the pro loses one, "Oh, he had a bit of tough luck." But when the amateur does it, they say, "Boy, did you see that sap choke?"

Whoever thinks the amateur has a patent on choking has another choking spell coming. Just because they deal you one of those PGA cards doesn't exempt you from "the Thing."

Choking, or "the Thing" as it has been described on tour, is a dreaded disease. And it doesn't play favorites. It can grab any man who walks on a golf course for money.

I've heard a lot of remedies for it. Some say to close your eyes and breathe deeply ten times. All that'll do for me is keep me alive. When I open those eyes, I'm standing there with that shot to hit and I'm still in as tough shape as I was before I got those ten deep breaths.

When "the Thing" grabs you out there, there's not much you can do. Your only thought is to get the ball away from you. Get it airborne, advance it. You know choking is tightening up. Your muscles become uncontrollable. Every club you pull out of the sack feels like the bag strap in your hands. It's wiggly, like a snake. You can't take the stick away from the ball. It is the most helpless feeling in the world.

I don't think there is a remedy for it once it has attacked a player; the best remedy is prevention. I feel that severe concentration is the remedy. Actually, in my mind it is a combination of lack of concentration and lack of confidence. A lot of players have golf swings that can take so much heat. Those swings have a breaking point. They have a chance to turn in a fine round, they miss one shot, and then "the Thing" swoops down and gets them. Their mind goes in circles, they can't concentrate on what they are supposed to do, and finally there's mental panic.

I remember Jimmy Demaret used to walk down the fairway shaking his arms furiously. Ole Jim was trying to get the blood circulating in them. It's true, when you choke, the muscles seem to actually cut off the blood to your hands.

What can happen to a man is that he begins thinking of what a particular shot, hole, or round of golf will mean to him if he succeeds. Therefore, he is thinking about all the things he should not be thinking about and so has gotten his mind off what he is supposed to be doing. Once that concentration is broken, anything can come into play.

But once, "the Thing" has you, you wish you were 1,000 miles away. The tournament doesn't mean anything, the shot is something you don't want to face. You say, "Man, I wish I was where my brother is and he was where I am." You wouldn't care if your brother was in Sing Sing.

I've done my share of choking, and I've seen players choke to death. I've seen them when they finally got the ball on the green and they'd sound like a bank teller counting change trying to get a dime out of their pocket to mark the ball. This is a pitiful sight.

You won't catch me dealing out any remedies for players who become victims of "the Thing" in the future—and it'll happen as long as they play the game of golf. But I can tell you that those players who concentrate hardest and longest are the ones who aren't apt to be gasping for those ten deep breaths and shaking their arms to get the blood flowing freely too often.

Once you learn to play championship golf, concentration is 75 percent of it after that. Palmer said that and Hogan proved it. And there you have two men "the Thing" didn't get to often. It stayed far away from Mr. Palmer and Mr. Hogan.

There have been times a player choked out there and got away with it. I mean he had such a lead that no one was able to run him down. But you can believe me, that player was honest with himself. He knew what had happened to him. You don't hear any of them saying, "I don't know whether I choked it or not." If they choked they knew it. It's unmistakable. Then it is time for that player to be honest with himself. He has to go back to the practice tee, get himself a swing that will take more heat, and teach himself to concentrate a bit harder. Did I say, "A bit harder?" Make that a helluva lot harder.

There's no way to outfight "the Thing" out there. But I'm sure there's a way to out-think it.

You keep referring to concentration. What is it and how important is it?

Once you've acquired a golf swing, then the rest of it depends on your ability to concentrate. After you have grooved that swing, concentration is 75 percent of golf. That's the reason I refer to it so often. It's important because it is 75 percent of my trade.

For golf professionals, concentration must start the moment the tournament starts. I mean when the first players move off that tee on Thursday, every player in the field had better be thinking about his golf game. If they are not, then they may not be around when the cut comes on Friday night. The fellow who can apply himself most to his work is the fellow who will win on Sunday night.

It was Byron Nelson, I believe, who put it as plainly as it could be put. He said he gave up competitive golf because the time came when he had to try to try. Byron meant nothing more than he was having trouble applying his complete concentration to his fine golf game and he knew his time had come.

I think that as fine a career as Dutch Harrison had, he would have been far better had he been able to apply himself mentally to his golf. But Dutch had too many things on his mind. When Dutch teed off, he was thinking about the nearby track, the daily double, would he be through in time to get his bet down? This hurt Dutch all his life. In my opinion, if Dutch had thought as much about golf as he did about the track he would have been right there with Ben Hogan. He could certainly have been that good.

I once asked Palmer what he thought he did best. He told me concentrate.

Take Hogan. He wrapped himself so tightly in his own business out there that he hardly knew who his playing partners were. He knew only when his turn came to hit. The late Clayton Heafner finished second to Hogan in a big tournament one year. Ben had shot a super last round to catch Clayt. After it was over, Heafner was telling about it.

"I wasn't playing with Ben, but word was drifting back to me that he was going great. I had it on my mind all day. Every chance I got I would look at the scoreboards to see how close he was coming to me. Finally, somewhere on the back nine he caught and passed me. There wasn't anything I could do about it. I was playing my best, he was just shooting the lights out.

"After it was over, I consoled myself that he had won the tournament, I hadn't lost it. I told myself second place wasn't the worst place to wind up. But then came the crusher; I was in the locker room, getting ready to go out to the presentation. Ben came striding down the corridor between the lockers. He was reading a telegram. We bumped shoulders, and he looked up and said: 'Oh, hi, Clayt, how'd it go today?'

"He was dead serious. He didn't even know that I had come close to winning the tournament. He proved right there that he'd paid far more attention to what he had been doing out there than I had to what I had been doing. When he asked me that question in the locker room, I knew then I had some concentration practicing ahead of me or I'd never again stay on the golf course with that little man."

And you can believe this or not, Heafner was known as one of the better concentrators in golf during his day. It simply points out that maybe Ben was the best of all of them.

But what is concentration? What are you supposed to do?

You are supposed to think of nothing but that next shot. You are supposed to picture what you want that shot to do. Your mind's eye—just like a moving picture show—is supposed to run that next shot across your brain for you. Then you are supposed to carry it out with your swing. This is supposed to occur the moment you tee the ball in the ground. It has to carry on with the iron shots and with each and every putt. You are supposed to see each shot as it is to be played. On the very good days, I have seen those twenty-foot putts roll into the cup seconds before I bent over the putt and rolled the thing in. And I'll promise you when the one that counted rolled in, it was nothing new to me. I had seen it before.

Okay, so you have played seven or eight holes and you have concentrated. You have envisioned every shot before you swung. You have made every effort to create reality from those visions— but nothing has gone right. So far that day your golf has been nothing more than a series of pretty visions and bad golf shots. What do you do now?

Well, the losers quit concentrating. This is the separating factor. This is when a lack of confidence creeps in and destroys the player's concentration. Usually you hear the player talk after it is all over. He says, "These fairways are the worst I have ever seen. They call these greens? Why, I had better greens for supper last night than they have on this golf course." The player is willing to give off any excuse rather than admit he was unable to concentrate for eighteen complete holes.

Maybe a distinction should be made here. The pros concentrate on these shots a bit differently than an amateur golfer would. The pro sizes up his lie, the playing conditions, wind and what not, distance, and then his mind's eye should envision what type of shot he should hit. Should it be a slightly hooked shot into the wind? A low one under the wind? Or must it be a pitch and run downwind? No matter, once he has envisioned the shot, he selects his club and goes about his business attempting to bring it off.

Many amateur players are not fortunate enough to be able to use these different shots. But that should not prevent them from envisioning some kind of shot to the green. It is as necessary for the amateur to picture his shot beforehand as it is for the professional. Somehow through the years this ability to concentrate on a shot has been termed "think positive" on the golf course. I have seen long instruction pieces written for amateurs in which the author suggests that if the amateur players "think positive" their results will be better.

I do not like that approach to this vital element of golf. It is definitely not thinking positive. It is concentrating on your work. The term "thinking positive" can bring in too many outside things. For instance, I've heard amateurs say, "Well, here's a par five. I'm going to think birdie on this hole." Well, he has had a positive thought, okay. But he is way ahead of himself. He must concentrate on each shot as it comes. This makes it a lot harder, I admit. But we are talking about a very difficult game, you know.

Long before television made the instant replay popular, golf professionals were suffering because there was such a thing in their mind's eye. Maybe a golfer would miss a short putt early in the round. A hole or two later he had another similar putt. Instead of seeing this one roll into the hole, he would think back to the first one. He would get an instant replay of the earlier one. He then makes some minor adjustment in his stroke and . . . oops . . . he's done it again.

There must be no instant replays. Once that mental picture is completed and the actual shot is made, it must be off to the next one. Good or bad, that last one should be dismissed and the mind applied to the next job.

I think back to the early part of 1970 when Gary Player came back to this country. There were some threats made against him and in several tournaments he had bodyguards. To my mind Gary showed an incredible ability to concentrate under these conditions. It is amazing to me that he did it. I don't see how anyone could think his way through a round wondering if he is going to be shot on the next swing. And think of the guys playing with Gary. They must have been wondering, if there really was someone out there ready to shoot Gary, then would they hit the right fellow? The way Gary played under those conditions proves a theory I've had for a long time. The greatest golf players in the world are the ones who are able to apply themselves mentally for the longest period of time.

It is impossible for a golf professional to be a winning player on tour if he has outside pressures weighing so heavily on him that they occupy his mind during a round. He must be so free of worry that there's nothing in the world more important than that next shot. These young players on tour today have caught on in a hurry. One thing they have that we didn't have when I started was freedom from financial worry. Most of them have adequate backing. Their job is to hit that golf ball and let the people at home worry about the money. And they know how to concentrate. Why, after the tournaments begin these days most of them are stuck for an answer if you say hello to them. They just drift around. They are in another world.

Years ago, we were expected to come off the golf course during the tournaments and socialize with the members in the clubhouse. Not today; these kids finish, grab a quick beer, and they're gone. Many of them head right to that practice tee and hit shots until they fall. The whole thing has become super commercial.

There were many times back in the old days when I would walk to the practice tee after a tournament round and hit balls for an hour. There was no one, just me and the caddie. I got a lot of good practice hours in that way. Not today. The practice area is littered with 100 or more players. The sky is black with divots as they lunge away at their practice shots. I haven't really made up my mind what they are practicing, but I know they must be concentrating on something because if you say something to them, you are lucky to get a grunt in return.

It should be pointed out there seem to be players on tour who defy the importance of concentration. By this I mean they seem to be too friendly with the gallery to have their minds completely on what they are doing.

Don't fool yourself. There's a pattern a golf professional can fall into that will permit him to be outwardly cordial to the gallery and at the same time be applying his subconscious mind to his golf. I have done this. The day I shot 60 at Hartford, Connecticut, I was jiving with the gallery all the way. But I never got my mind off what I wanted to do with those clubs and that ball. When time came for me to hit, my mind fell right back on what I was supposed to be doing. This is mental discipline. It is something that cannot be trusted, however. There have been days when I tried to jive with the gallery; one of them would ask something too personal or distracting and I was done for the day. Need I remind you that I let them know it on the spot?

Lee Trevino has remarkable mental discipline. He appears to be carrying on with the gallery all the time. There are few people around who don't like and admire this little man. He carries on his jiving right after a shot. He knows he has time to walk to the next one. He knows he has time to reapply himself. For instance, the crowd loves to see Lee bang an iron shot straight at the pin. Many times he'll yell, "Don't move, hole!" This is color. The fans appreciate colorful comments like this. But Lee hasn't done his concentration any harm. He has time before he has to play another shot. And believe me, his mind is so disciplined that he'll be concentrating on that putt.

Palmer wasn't so free and easy out there either. Oh, there were times when he'd walk up to his ball and someone would say, "Arnie, you'd better thank this man. Your ball hit him and bounced back into the fairway." Palmer turned to the guy and gave him that little grin. The guy couldn't have been happier with $1,000—Palmer made this guy's tournament. Then maybe Arnold would chip the thing on the green, hole the putt for a birdie, and toss the ball to the guy. Well, then you could up that $1,000 to $10,000. Arnie had trapped all of them then, but he hadn't allowed the incident to rupture his concentration.

Several years ago, a tour player met this girl during one of our stops in Canada. They dated a couple of nights and maybe to make the way easier for himself, the player promised the girl he would send for her and take her along with him on tour. On the final night he was in town, he told her to quit her job and join him the next week in Milwaukee. He didn't mean any of this. He was doing it because he felt she wanted to hear it and maybe to soothe his own conscience.

On the next Thursday, our hero was playing the eighth hole at Milwaukee. He was two under par, going real good. Suddenly, he looked in the woods and there, tramping through the weeds, a suitcase in either hand and a big smile on her face, was the Canadian girl friend. I will let the player tell the rest of the story:

"I was done. When I saw her, I first looked for a place to run. I actually started to head out through the woods on the other side. But then I made myself walk over to her. Sure enough, she told me she had quit her job and had come down to join me for the rest of the year. I told her to go back up to the clubhouse and wait for me. I told her I had about two more hours on the course."

Little did he know. He had two more holes. He shanked his second shot and made eight on the eighth hole. On the ninth hole, he made seven. He finished the nine holes, 41. He reported a severe pain in his shoulder to the officials and was permitted to withdraw.

I bring up this story simply to point out that sometimes even that subconscious mind can't do the concentrating when the distraction is major.

It is in times like these that what Byron Nelson said rings so true: "There's no use going out there when you have to try to try."

The characters! Haven't you met some dillies
in twenty-five years on tour?

There's one thing wrong with the question. Too bad someone else isn't answering it. I know I would probably head that list. I'd love to read what they had to say about me.

I admit that some of the things I did and still do at those tournaments would be termed peculiar.

I would go to the course on a particular day feeling my pilot light was burning low. I thought I needed something to get it going good. I have to have somebody to get me fired for the round. On the first tee, there is usually a PGA official who announces the players, and when that is done he'd say, "Play away, Mr. Bolt."

There have been times when I would look over my shoulder and answer back, "Don't you tell me to hit until I'm ready. I don't need one of you guys rushing me." Then I'd stand there and stare at the poor fellow. I can't remember one of them ever answering me.

But there was a reason I'd stand there. I knew the minute I jumped the fellow, the fans would be scurrying around. They'd be off to the practice green, some would go as far as the clubhouse. They would find friends and tell them, "Hey, Bolt is right today. He hasn't struck the first ball and he has hung the PGA official out to dry." I'd pick up a pretty good gallery then.

That fires me up some. The more people out there to watch me hit good shots, the more good shots I hit.

There was a fellow out there named Ivan Gantz. He was from the Chicago area.

Ivan could play pretty good golf at times. But, like the rest of us, he wanted to play good golf all the time. Ivan had this one habit that few fans saw, but was common knowledge to the players. If he'd miss a tee shot, he would back off in the crowd and stomp hell out of his driver. The head of his driver looked like all the termites in the world had gathered right there for lunch. You couldn't have found one like it in any used-club barrel in the country.

When I first saw Ivan do this, I couldn't believe that a man would treat one of his best friends this way. I never had a driver I didn't hold in the same esteem I held my own life. My driver was my golf game.

However, there came a day. I had played ten or twelve holes and things hadn't gone right. I walked up on a tee, aimed the jewel down the middle and dropped it off in the trash somewhere out there on the right side. I knew I had made me another bogey if I played real good.

As I backed off the tee, permitting the other members of the group to drive, I thought of old Ivan. I looked down at the shiny head of my driver and I thought of Ivan again. Then I looked at my left foot. If I dug real hard with my left foot, I could put some termite holes through the shoe and into my skin. After all, the driver had little to do with the way I tortured that golf ball. But, I thought quickly, I had never seen Ivan stomp his left foot. And the foot wasn't really to blame, either. How does a guy stomp his brains out?

Once again I looked down at that shiny head. I dropped back off the tee, away from the fans who were watching the others hit. Then I stomped.

60

Evidently, I hadn't learned my lesson well. Later I found that Ivan stomped with just the toe of his shoe, never the heel. I stomped with the heel. The spikes had gone so deeply into the head of the club I could not pull it off. Now the players and fans were moving down the fairway and there I was, back behind the tee, wearing this golf club for a right shoe.

As they walked away from me, I guess "the Thing" grabbed me. I choked. I could see the next group coming up to the tee and finding me lying there with this club fixed to my shoe. I yelled, "Hey, help me. Help me."

One of the players rushed back, he thought I'd had a heart attack. All he could see was me lying there trying to kick that club off my foot. I mumbled something like, "Ivan, you know Ivan Gantz does it. Damn Ivan Gantz."

The player soon discovered what was wrong. He snatched the club off my foot. As we walked down the fairway, hurrying to catch the other players, I noticed he was giving me plenty of room. When we had reached the safety of the gallery, he turned and asked, "Who's Ivan Gantz?"

Embarrassed, I yelled, "Hell, man, you don't know Ivan Gantz? He's a helluva player."

There weren't too many things Ivan could do with a golf club that I couldn't. But there was something he could do with a golf shoe I couldn't master.

You can't talk of the colorful people of golf without mentioning Ed Oliver. The old-timers will remember Ed. I mean the old-time chefs, waiters, and waitresses. I thought the world of the guy. He's passed away now. He was on tour after the war right up until the mid-1950s.

Ed was about 5 feet 11 inches and went from 260 to 280 pounds. His weight depended on the heat that particular week. It's amazing that I remember that his name was Ed. I never called him that in my life. I'll bet that if anybody did, he wouldn't have answered. They called him Porky for a while. I called him Pork Chops at first. Then I cut it down to just Chops. He'd answer to either Porky or Chops.

At most tournaments, the officials would sell scrip books. Cash wasn't any good at the club. If you wanted to eat, you would have to buy books of scrip. The players always got them at a discount. But we'd see Chops heading into the dining room with just one book in his hand and we'd get out of there as if someone had yelled fire. We knew one book wouldn't get Chops through a meal. He'd have to borrow some scrip from somebody. As we'd head through the door, someone would say, "Man, I feel like I already saved caddie fee for the week."

I think Chops got on several diets during the years he was on tour. I say, I think he did. There was never any evidence. Some of the guys say he went on diets because he had such a good time getting off of them. After he had been on one of these diets for a week or so, the guys would start pulling for him. "Porky is doing better this time," they would say. "He hasn't faltered but one time. A couple of nights ago he ate a butcher's shop."

As long as I can remember, golf has had trick-shot artists. I know of three who got national acclaim—Joe Kirkwood, Sr., the Marvelous Montague (John), and Paul Hahn.

I didn't see Kirkwood much. I think I caught his act a couple of times. But I saw Hahn both as a tour player and as a trick shooter. Montague, I didn't pay much attention to him. He'd come out there with a rake, a hoe, and a shovel. That's the way he played his round. I used to whisper to other players while he was putting on his act, "The Marvelous Montague, my ass. . . . Why don't they call him Farmer John?"

He wasn't kidding me. I knew he'd have loved nothing better than to have swapped that rake, hoe, and shovel for some of those real sticks and some of that competition . . . and some of that cheese they passed out on Sunday. But he had a gimmick.

62

He tried with it. I guess there were some fans who liked to watch him beat that dude around with the farmware.

The thing I recall about Kirkwood, Sr., the most was his finale. He'd end his act by asking for a volunteer from the gallery. It was always some wide-eyed Negro boy, thirteen, fourteen or fifteen years old. Joe would announce that he was going to hit some shots down the fairway and if the boy could keep from getting hit, then he'd give him $5. At first, the volunteer would be leery. He thought maybe Joe was going to put him 10 to 15 yards out. No. Joe would permit him to get 150 to 160 yards away. This seemed easy. The kid would go for it in a minute.

Joe was a helluva one-iron player. He could drill that walking cane straight as a string. And that club is strictly for killing snakes. It doesn't have any loft. You can't hit the ball high with it. Joe had it figured good. He knew that when the shot got 150 yards away it would be six or seven feet off the ground. He knew that if the youngster stood in that close he wouldn't get hit. But to the boy standing out that far, he'd see that ball leave the clubhead low and now! It must have looked as if every shot was going to hit him in the head. All the kids Joe put out there would stare the first two or three shots down. Maybe they would fall to earth as the ball zoomed over their heads. But they would stay in the same place. The fans would laugh and oooohhhh and aaaahhhh.

I think the reaction of the fans would soon take over. The kids would hear this and think maybe the balls were coming too close to them. Then the action would start. They would start running left or right. Joe could slice or hook the club. If the boy headed right, Joe would slice the ball and the kid found himself heading right into it. Then he would head left and Joe would hook. The kid couldn't move but what he had a one-iron coming at him. The act was over when the boy hit the ground and just lay there. Joe would then run out to him, pat him on the head, and give him the cash.

Hahn is the Number One trick-shot man in the world today.

And I mean world because there aren't many places in the world Paul hasn't hit slices and hooks. There are a lot of places in the world he hasn't hit straight balls.

Paul used to play the tour. I remember his last try out there. It was in Milwaukee in the early 1950s. He had a club job out in the Midwest somewhere and took his shot at the tour now and then. This was a period when he was hitting "trick" shots but wasn't billed as a trick-shot artist and wasn't getting anything but cut from the field for hitting them. After this particular tournament, Paul announced that it was his last. "I'm going to find me something else," he said.

He was smart. He went to the thing he could do best, hit snipe hooks and slices. Someone told me he eventually got Bob Hope's writers to write his script for him. That, combined with his natural talent for delivery, made him a hit. He can strap some chatter on you. And he can strap some hooks and slices on you, too.

There's a fellow who played with us out there a long while who I think deserves far more recognition than he got.

It's hard to list Ed Furgol here with some of the other characters of the tour, because there was a year there, 1954, when Ed was the best golfer in the world. He won the National Open that year. Man, could he drive that golf ball. His drives left those tees like they were late for supper. During his childhood, Ed fell from a playground swing and broke his left arm. Something went wrong and the arm never grew. It was small in the biceps and crooked. When he walked, it sort of flapped out away from his body.

Let me say here that in those days on tour we were a closer knit bunch of guys than these kids are today. I'm not saying that everybody liked everybody else, but I'm saying that there was a closer brotherhood back fifteen years ago. I explain this because Ed Furgol acquired the nickname of "Wingy" and it wasn't that anyone was teasing him about his withered arm. It was just that he carried it out away from his body and it reminded you of a wing. Nobody could tease Ed, anyhow. If they did, they'd look up there Sunday and there he was getting $300 to $400 more money. Besides, how are you going to kid a guy who won the National Open?

I don't think the PGA ever knew how much of an inspiration Ed Furgol was to fans as we toured the country. If the association did realize it, it never publicized the fact that here was a man who had overcome a horrible handicap to become one of the greatest golfers on tour. The PGA was satisfied to let Ed do the best he could with what he had to work with. If he made it, he got his money. If he didn't, "We'll see you later." But that was okay with Ed. He had worked harder than most people building himself a golf game despite his withered arm. And he asked no favors. The thing I liked about him was that he never whispered about the PGA, the players, or anything that he didn't like. If he thought it was wrong, he'd say it.

I remember that he was a club pro when he won the Open. He had a club in St. Louis. That was a great feat in itself. You don't find many club pros winning the National Open. It usually takes a man who is conditioned to the competition. But Ed came right out from behind that pro-shop counter and won the big one.

People didn't realize, I guess, what this can do for a club. At least the people at Ed's Westwood Country Club didn't. Westwood's membership reacted as if Ed had done nothing at all. Oh, I think they had a small dinner for him. And I think they did give him a $1,000 Savings Bond. But many other clubs did far more for their professionals than that and those pros had done much less than Ed.

Anyway, Wingy didn't hang around there long after his wonderful victory. And he was quick to tell people why he left. "How can you stay with those people," he said. "I won the National Open, I'm their pro, and they acted like it happened every day. Sure, they gave me a Savings Bond, something you can buy wholesale."

Wonder what the PGA has done for this gutsy little guy who served as an inspiration to the thousands of handicapped fans all over the country?

Why has golf forgotten Frank Stranahan? I wonder if the hundreds of guys "Mus" helped out there still remember what he did for them?

I called him Mus. His nickname was Muscles. He lifted weights between tournaments. He took them with him in a suitcase. They say that Mus used to pull up to a hotel, grab his weight suitcase in one hand, his clothes suitcase in the other, and move right up to the check-in counter. After he checked in, the clerk would ring for a bellboy and Mus would grab the clothes suitcase and head for the elevator. He would turn just in time to see the bellboy get blue in the face trying to lift that bag with the weights in it. He's left a bunch of them lying there with a double hernia.

Frank played the tour a long time as an amateur. His family had a little something in Toledo, Ohio, going for them called Champion Spark Plugs. In his later years, Frank turned pro. But I remember the days when he was an amateur, giving us pros hell.

At first his desire was to win everything there was to win as an amateur. He was going to make them forget Bobby Jones. And there was a time when I thought he could have done it. But he was in too big a hurry. If Mus thought someone had something to teach about the golf game, he wanted it. He'd go anywhere, see anybody if he thought they could help him. The end result was that he became confused. At one time there he had fourteen swings for fourteen clubs.

But he was great when he was going good. The guys used to love to have him walking around out there with those Italian silk trousers, those cashmere sweaters, and those pretty shirts. He could always dig his hand in that sock and come up with some cash for a guy who was down on his luck. They didn't mind asking Frank, and he didn't hesitate to help them if he thought they had a chance.

He was a show on the golf course. They'd let colleges (women's colleges) out for the week when he hit town. You'd see little college girls out there who didn't know the difference between a golf ball and a spark plug. But they'd be right on Mus' heels all the way. He had the poses, too. He'd lean on those clubs with that 30-inch waist and stick out that 46-inch chest and flex those big biceps and you could hear the giggles. Those were the days gals went for physical development rather than the sandals, long hair, and malnutrition of today.

During one spell when Mus was an amateur, Jack Burke and I used to put on a lot of exhibitions around Texas. Mus would beg us to let him play with us. He couldn't collect money for it, he was an amateur. Fact is, it would cost him money traveling. But he loved it. He begged us. We'd kid him along and then we'd tell him it was okay. Jack and I would fly. Mus would jump in that big Lincoln of his and beat us there. There was a time when Mus could pump up those muscles and hit it with anybody in the world.

Right after the war and for some years later, there was a man on tour who probably hit more golf balls than anybody who ever lived. Let me put it this way, George Schoux hit more golf balls than he ever should have.

Someone once told me that they saw George standing under a tree at a Chicago golf club. "What you doing there, George?" the man asked.

"Reading a little poetry," said George. And there he was, standing under a tree reading poetry.

But! The cover of the book was bloody. George's hands were bloody. He had been hitting golf balls so long that day that his hands had started bleeding. He was reading poetry until the blood hardened and he could go back to hitting golf shots.

George could play a little bit. But he was so dedicated to becoming the greatest player in the world that he never really had a chance. Many times he hit balls until his hands would stand no more. But as soon as the blood hardened enough so that the club wouldn't slip, he'd be back out there.

Last I heard of George, he was a patient in a rest home in California. The story goes that they found the perfect cure for him. The hospital owned a golf course and they let George work there as a professional.

Why is the tour short on retirement parties?

I can't think of any tour golfer who held a press conference and said, "Here it is, gentlemen. The old golf bag is hung there in the garage. I'm through."

You talk about old soldiers not dying, but just fading away, try pro golf players. They don't exactly "fade" away, some of them outright slice away and others hook away.

But there is nothing ceremonious about the way they go. They usually are honest with themselves. They know when the tour becomes too rough. They know when their legs or nerves have run their course. They just quit competing in tour events.

On the other hand, some of the former tour stars can still play very good golf, as evidenced by the fact that there are some excellent professional events for players over fifty years of age.

However, that wasn't exactly a senior tournament they held down at Palm Beach Gardens in February. It was the PGA Championship. I finished third there. If I had held any thoughts of formally retiring from the tour, they would have ended that Sunday when only Nicklaus and Casper beat me out for the PGA title.

You remember the great job Sam Snead did at Westchester in

July. Sam finished fourth in that one. He's fifty-nine. He joked with them up there about how he should be home mowing the lawn instead of competing with the young players in tournament golf. But believe me, it was just a joke. Sam will be showing up out there as long as he can walk seventy-two holes.

He also made a reference to nerves. He said if there were only some way to get transplants of nineteen-year-old nerves, he and Ben Hogan could still win on tour. Well, the nerves may cost the older players strokes. But you can still rank a professional golfer with bad nerves right up there with the bravest mountain climbers and best brain surgeons.

I have gone through this before. Successful tour professionals are long on nerve and courage.

People make a big thing of George Blanda of the Oakland Raiders kicking extra points and field goals at the age of forty-four. Or Hoyt Wilhelm going in a major league game to relieve at forty-five. Well, those fellows on tour can be glad that Snead isn't forty-four years old. Look what he can do at fifty-nine. The year he was forty-four, he finished Number 7 on the money list.

In late July, 1971, they played the PGA Better Ball Championship at the Laurel Valley Country Club, Ligonier, Pennsylvania. This is a long, tough course. It rained out Thursday's round, so the tournament committee set up two rounds on Sunday. Now on Sunday, it rained twice. But there was fifty-one-year-old Julius Boros walking thirty-six holes, finishing second in the event with his partner Bill Collins.

And there, again, was Sam Snead—fifty-nine, mind you— walking thirty-six holes over a soggy golf course, getting drenched one minute, drying out and getting drenched again. If there had ever been a time for guys to retire because of age, Boros and Snead came face to face with theirs on that day.

In March of 1971, I called my friend Lloyd Ferrentino of the Bardmoor Country Club in St. Petersburg, Florida, and asked if he'd like to have Ben Hogan play an exhibition there. Ferrentino's reaction was so fast that next thing I knew it was two weeks from the time I had presented the plan, Ben and I were on the Bardmoor practice tee, and close to 4,000 fans were there to see the Little Man at work.

Some years ago, Ben had agreed to play an exhibition match with me. But shortly before we were to play, he hurt his shoulder and had to drop out. He told me at that time that he owed me one. But I had never planned to hold him to it.

Ben is not one you have to hold to anything. He felt he owed it to me and he agreed to it. You realize, you don't have to be a golf nut to know that Ben Hogan doesn't play too many exhibition matches. In fact, the one he and I played at Bardmoor was his first in ten years.

Ben's appearance today—he's fifty-eight—belies the fact that he was involved in that head-on collision with a Greyhound bus. I said his appearance belies it. His walk does not. He still limps. And he lives in constant fear that his left knee will collapse on him.

"Actually," he told me, "I need an operation on the knee. But I'm not going to have it. I've faced enough knives." He described the aching in that left knee as, "feeling as if someone were stabbing me with an ice pick. Or as I think it would feel to be stabbed with an ice pick."

We offered to let him ride an electric cart during the exhibition. He shook his head and said, "I'll walk as long as I can."

At the third hole, Ben's knee gave way just as he came through his swing off the tee. Not everyone knew it. But I saw it immediately and he confirmed it as we walked down the fairway. I asked him if he wanted me to get him a cart. He said that he would try walking at least nine holes.

When we finished nine, he walked right over to the 10th tee and waited for me to hit. I knew there wasn't any sense in me suggesting the cart again. I just kept playing and shut up about it.

It was the first time Ben had ever played the Bardmoor course. The course isn't difficult, but the greens are so large you must be precise in your club selection in order to have short birdie putts.

What I'm saying is, you can play Bardmoor, hit fifteen, sixteen, or seventeen greens and still shoot no better than par. Though you hit the greens, you still have putts of 30-40 feet, hardly birdie putts.

Ben had the ball within the 15-foot birdie range nine times that afternoon. Pretty good for a fifty-eight-year-old on a strange course with a painful knee. However, after he finished he described his even par round as "terrible."

It was so "terrible" that those fans around the eighteenth hole gave him a standing ovation when he walked up on the eighteenth green, and the St. Petersburg *Evening Independent* ran a six-column-24-inch picture of him the next afternoon.

They all but begged him to come back and play again next year.

One thing about the exhibition match I recall more than any other was the thirteenth hole. There's a large hill off the thirteenth about 200 yards from the tee. This hill hides the green.

When we reached the tee, Ben asked me, "Which way?"

"See that fellow out there with the red shirt," I said, indicating a man standing on that hill. "Hit it right over his head."

Just as Ben was approaching the ball, the man I had pointed to began walking toward the green. "Hey," I said, "he's leaving. Don't walk away."

Ben smiled and said, "It's okay. I have the spot."

And did he have it. He drilled the ball perfectly over the spot the fellow had left. The fans around the thirteenth tee knew full well why there had never been a retirement party for Ben Hogan.

Many of the old-time stars who played in the early 1950s with Ben, Boros, Snead, and me have quietly faded, sliced or hooked away. But most of them are still in golf somewhere, somehow.

And I didn't attend a single retirement party.

Whenever I can, I steal the old vaudeville line. Someone will say, "Tom, have you played golf this well all your life?"

I answer, "Not yet."

Mr. Bolt, were you born with that fluid golf swing?

I'd be lying if I didn't tell you I wish I had been. But I'd be lying if I told you I had been.

Truth is, I was thirty-eight years old when I finally gave up on finding a swing of my own and asked Ben Hogan to help me. Older than that if it is true what they say about duck hooks aging a fellow.

Ben and I had played a round of golf in Ben's hometown of Fort Worth. When we were done, I asked Ben if it would be okay for me to come back to Fort Worth and spend some time with him.

Now this is something just everyone doesn't ask Ben Hogan. He could have said, "Yeah, yeah! We'll get together sometime." That would have been the end of that. And, I suspect, the end of me. But Ben and I had been pretty close friends all the way. I imagine my voice had the desperation of a guy lying five buried in the lip of a trap. Ben told me to come back anytime. Anytime was two weeks later.

This was sort of a Peeping Tom lesson. He told me a few things, shoved my left hand over on top of the club, and sent me out playing. I played with the members around that tough Colonial Country Club every day for a week. First thing I knew, I was playing par or better every time. Ben wouldn't play along, but I'd catch him hiding behind bushes, peeping out to see me swing at the ball. Occasionally he would ride up in an electric cart and have me hit two or three shots for him. He'd never say a word. Just ride up, nod for me to hit a couple of shots. I'd rifle them toward a green and he would disappear just as he'd arrived.

I've always said that Hogan knew more about hitting a golf ball than any five of the top golf professionals in the world. He's the only player I have ever known to get an ovation from the fans on the practice tee. I've seen him playing practice rounds before a tournament and half his gallery was made up of other professionals. I've played eighteen holes of golf with him when he hit every

72

shot at the flag. I mean every shot went straight at the flag, the only flaw in the round was either his shots were fifteen feet too long or fifteen feet too short—but dead on target.

He's not one to waste words. He wastes as many words as he does golf shots. So when he never said a word to me when I hit those shots for him, I had enough faith in him to believe he would have told me had I been doing something wrong. In fact, it was four years later before I knew that I had actually absorbed what he had tried to teach me in that week.

When the Memphis Open of 1960 ended, Ben, myself, and Gene Littler had tied. We met in an eighteen-hole playoff. Oh, did I want to beat Hogan. All week long we had been kidding each other. I had told him, "Little Man, when I get you out there this week, I'm going to bring you home. You'll belong to me when Sunday night comes."

Well, it hadn't worked out quite that way. Sunday night had come and gone. Here it was midday Monday and I still had Hogan, plus Littler, to dispose of. A fellow suddenly knows how David felt with his slingshot. But, like David, I was a dead-eye for nine holes. At the halfway point, I was 32, Ben was 36, and Littler was 38. It took Ben just seven holes to undo what I'd done to him in nine holes. We walked to the seventeenth tee dead even. He and Gene both had just birdied the sixteenth hole, and I don't mind telling you it seemed like an hour on the seventeenth tee before it came time for me to hit. I was the last player in the threesome.

The seventeenth is a par three. That day it played extra long. Ben and Gene hit three-irons. Both were on the green, but short some fifteen to twenty feet. As I walked to my bag, I thought, "Hell, they're not up." I thumbed through the sack for my two-iron. As I took the club back, I thought to myself, "It's now or never."

With that left hand riding high, just as Ben had taught me, I put the prettiest swing on that two-iron you have ever seen. The ball never left the flag. It was smoked. The shot landed six or eight feet from the cup, skidded to a halt.

Now all the people were yelling and clapping. It was noisy as the devil. But despite all the noise, all the confusion, when Ben said, "Nice shot!" it was like a double clap of thunder to me. It was the only thing he had said to me all day.

For the historians, I made that putt on the seventeenth, tied the final hole, and wore the Memphis Open crown for a year. But what was worth more than the crown or the money was Ben saying, "Nice shot!" just once. That's enough psychological therapy to last a golfer six months.

A quick riddle for you, Tom. What has fifteen heads and one brain?

You want me to say a professional golfer, don't you?

I'm not going to say it. It isn't the exact answer. The answer is a successful professional golfer. Too many times you find nothing but fifteen heads running around out there—fourteen of them in the bag and the other one doing nothing more than hurting the chances those official fourteen would have in a thinking man's hands.

Let me run through my bag of friends for you. First, get it clear we are talking about a windless day. There are other conditions that enter into the picture. I will attempt to explain them as I go along. At the end I will talk a bit about wind, the course, and the player.

The driver: The good golf professional has to be prepared for the soft, lush fairways and the hard, bare fairways. On the lush course he must be prepared to hit the ball high, getting most of his distance in the air. If he is a player who hits those low drillers he will suffer plenty on a lush course. I can adapt my tee shots to different fairways. Most anywhere I play I can depend on 250-yard tee shots. And I will keep the little jewel in play.

Nine-iron: My average is 115 to 125 yards. I never try to hit my nine-iron more than 125 yards. Many times I will use it rather than the wedge for shots under 115 yards. My thinking on this club is a smooth, controlled swing. I always try to remember that it is easier to hit this club easy than it is to hit it hard.

Eight-iron: Usually, anything from 125 yards to 140 yards is played with an eight-iron. But I must tell you that there have been many times when I've hit my eight-iron when the shot actually called for the nine. I do this to stress the fact that I must swing easy. If there is doubt, then I will take the stronger club. My aim with all iron shots is to hit the ball to the hole. I'm not one of those guys who plays fifteen to twenty feet short of the hole and hopes the ball bounces close to the cup. I try to put the ball into the cup on the fly. It must be the basketball player in me. But I know if I hit the shot correctly, the backspin will stop the ball close to the hole if I carry it far enough. On these shots I try to have two of those fifteen heads working toward one goal. The head that controls the swinging uses judgment enough to select the proper club. The head of the club applies the spin to stop the ball. You'd be surprised how many times the metal head of the golf club does its job far better than the head resting on the shoulders of a human being. Sort of scares you, doesn't it?

Seven-iron: Now we have come to my old friend. For the record, I attempt to use a seven-iron for shots from 140 to 150 yards. But I must confess that I have probably made more errors with this club than any in my bag. And, believe it or not, it is my favorite club. Don't ask me why, but most touring professionals have a particular club that they like to use. My favorite happens to be the seven-iron. Many times I have stood out there knowing full well that the shot called for a six-iron. But the longer Old Dad stood there, the easier it was for me to convince myself that I could reach the green with the seven. "Just hit it a little firmer," I'd tell myself as I drew it from the sack. Right there, the tempo I strive for throughout every swing has been destroyed. I'm trying to do something with a seven-iron that could be done simply with a six-iron and the proper tempo. But, as I say, I love to hit seven-iron shots. The favoritism I show this one club has caused me to hit many forced shots with it. This in turn has caused me some bad moments. You guessed it, I have thrown a seven-iron or two in my time.

Six-iron: This is the last of the scoring irons. By that I mean that successful golf professionals feel that any time they have a six-, seven-, eight- or nine-iron to the green, then they feel they should hit it to within six to ten feet of the hole. I usually allow myself 150 to 160 yards with the six-iron. I should point out now that I know the exact distances I can hit all these clubs. Also, I am blessed with pretty good eyesight. I can judge pretty near the exact distance I am from a flag stick. I'm not talking about how far I am from the green, mind you. I'm talking about from the cup. Every time I get me a new set of clubs, I find me a nice, wide open place to practice with them. I walk off every yard of the practice area. I know exactly how far I can hit each club. I hit hundreds and hundreds of shots. Then, when I go to the course, I depend on my eyes, not my legs, to tell me how far it is from the position of the ball to the hole. I can't understand why these kids on tour today walk off those distances. You'll see them walk from their ball toward the green, or back toward some object they have measured prior to the tournament. Then they come back to their shot and lash at it with an awful swing. If you saw Hogan do this, you could understand. He is a precisioned golfer. But he never did. I played with Palmer not long ago, he didn't do it either. Neither does Sam Snead. Nearly all the great players played by sight and feel, not by walking and mumbling to themselves.

Five-iron: I use this club for shots of 160 to 170 yards. There have been and are players today who regard the five-iron as I do the six, a scoring iron. They feel that if they can reach the pin with a five-iron then they will be accurate enough to hit the ball to within six to ten feet. I don't feel as if I can hit the five-iron as close to the hole as I can my six-, seven-, eight- or nine-irons. I couldn't honestly regard this as a scoring club. It's good to know you can smack the five-iron up and over all the trouble around a green. Get it back there ten to twenty feet of the joint every time and you are going to make some of those putts.

Rapidly now, I will take these long irons in order. I use the four-iron for shots of 170 to 180 yards; the three-iron for shots of 180 to 190 yards, and the two-iron up to 200 yards.

For shots longer than this, pros vary.

Some of them—Julius Boros and Sam Snead come to mind—use one-irons. I can't recommend this club. Boros and Snead are wonders with it. But both of them have put in years of practice. You must have a good, fluid swing to make that club pay off. If I catch one of my amateur friends playing with a one-iron he had better be putting with it.

I have two choices for shots more than 200 yards. One is the three-wood and the other is the five-wood or my Medicare club. I call it that because these days you see a lot of amateur senior golfers using five-woods instead of long irons. It is not a bad idea.

Let's back up just a moment. I would like to point out that it is the hardest thing in the world for a player, even a pro, to imagine that with the very same smooth swing he applies to a nine-iron for a shot of 115 yards, he can hit a four-iron 175 yards. Or, he can hit a three-iron 185 yards, or a two-iron 195 yards. The tendency is to swing too hard with these long irons. You have robbed yourself of power.

There, you have gotten me talking about what those fifteen heads should do on a perfectly calm day. But what happens when the wind blows? What happens when you hit off bare ground? Or when you hit from sand? Or when you hit from deep rough?

There are days when the wind is blowing in your face, from behind or from the left or right. These are variables which separate the great golfers from the so-so players. How well equipped to handle these situations are you?

I have long preached that the amateur players are much better off hooking the ball than fading it. Only the pros should fade the ball. For the uninitiated, hooking means hitting the ball

77

so that it will approach its target from a right-to-left angle. Fading is hitting the ball from left to right.

Nothing ever scared Hogan on a golf course. But there was one type shot he did not care for. That was the iron to the green when the wind was blowing over his left shoulder. Ben disliked that shot and I dislike it. It just seemed to us that when the wind was coming from the left, we never could start the ball far enough left. This is a shot both of us have spent hours and hours practicing.

Personally, I would rather play into the wind than downwind. Whenever I go out to practice, I always try to hit into the wind. I can tell more about how I'm swinging when I watch the ball travel into the wind.

The successful golf player cannot depend on perfect weather, a perfect lie, or perfect club selection each time he goes on a golf course. Therefore, he must arm himself with hundreds of types of shots. This is why it is so important for a golf professional to have excellent concentration. He knows so many shots. He must first decide on what type of shot to hit, then with what club, and then picture the ball flying exactly that way. The clubhead is made to execute the shot. The player's head must believe it can be done.

Is the touring pro dressed for his round of golf if he forgets to bring his pillbox with him?

With some of them, golf is a game of three P's. Putts, pars, and pills.

Let's not take one step off the first tee without me first saying that, yes, I have tried pills and playing golf. I haven't tried the heavy stuff, just tranquilizers. I tried them with the idea that they'd enable me to forget everything but what I was trying to do at the time—that, of course, being to bury that white jewel in eight inches of iron eighteen times in as few swings as I could take.

I soon found that Tranquilized Tommy didn't play the game nearly as well as Terrible-Tempered Tommy. Instead of aiding me to concentrate on my golf, they did nothing but make me concentrate on getting off the golf course and resting. They relaxed me to a point that I just about snored between golf shots.

Just as the game itself has changed in the twenty-five years since I turned professional, so have the means with which the players try to improve themselves. Back when I first started you could recognize the players not only by their swings, but by the drinks they ordered at the country club bars. Twenty years ago they could have blindfolded me, placed me at one end of the bar, read the drink orders, and I could have told you who was in the room. There was Martini Mac, Manhattan Mike, Scotch-on-rocks Robert and so on. Not all of the players drank, but most of them did. And believe me, a man had to be pretty good not to become an alcoholic on tour. Just think, we moved from city to city from January through November. It was routine to us, but a big thing to the city we visited. They really put on the dog at the clubs we'd visit.

In those early days, the pros didn't mind staying around the club bar after their rounds. They don't do that too much today. It was nothing for a group of members to start buying drinks at five every afternoon for any of the players who wanted to share in the revelry. That would go on to maybe nine or ten o'clock and then perhaps, as an afterthought, someone would mention dinner. They would or would not eat, depending on the amount they had to drink. It would be interesting to know just how many honest to goodness winning golf players rattled their careers around in cocktail glasses with three lumps of ice.

The idea that six-year-old whiskey could give a twenty-five-year-old golf pro two a side and win the match never dawned on hundreds of young players who never really understood how final that "friend" was being when he said, "Aw, c'mon, have one more for the road." Too many of those young pros of years ago read too much about the great Walter Hagen. They read and believed too much.

Walter has passed away. But his legend remains. He was one of the great, great men of our sport. Not only was he known as the King of the Fairways, but he was also saluted as the King of the Clubhouse. Scotch-and-water Walter was the center of attraction everywhere he traveled. Though he was seldom seen without a drink in his hand, those who were close to him will tell you that he hardly ever finished a full drink. He'd leave half a glass lying here, half a glass lying there. He was merrymaking, okay, but he wasn't consuming the amount of alcohol people thought he was.

Walter was not one who thought that tossing and turning in bed, fretting over tomorrow's match, was a way to prepare oneself for golf. During the PGA Match Play Championship one year, the bartender at the host club happened to be a Hagen fan. On the eve of a critical semifinal match, it was near midnight and Sir Walter was holding court on the bar stool.

"Mr. Hagen," said the bartender in almost a whisper, "don't you think you've been here long enough? You know, your opponent went to bed three hours ago."

Hagen smiled, acknowledging the good intentions of the fan and answered, "Young man, he may have gone to bed three hours ago. But he knows who he is playing. You can rest assured that he hasn't slept a wink."

Just as history tells us that the golfer who beat Walter Hagen to bed that night by four hours still was four holes short the next day, history also tells us that Walter Hagen was not a man who drank his golf career away. He was not a man another golfer should pattern himself by off the course. Just as he knew how to handle all types of golf shots, Walter knew, also, how to handle himself.

If there is a Walter Hagen among us today, it would be Lee Trevino. Here is a young man who handles his business on and off the course as well as Hagen did—or just about as well. I'm not telling tales out of school when I recall Lee's exploits of early 1970 in Miami. At the press conference after the National Airlines Open, Lee told newsmen that he thought he was lucky to win. "I went to the jai alai matches last night," he said. "A friend and I drank doubles between each game." Asked how many doubles he drank, Lee snapped, "Well, how many games do they have?"

They had twelve jai alai games that night.

Lee and I were paired together in the CBS Golf Classic, the year I made the comment on national television that Joe Dey should do something about players taking pills. I guess everybody thought I was kidding all the way. I wasn't.

After one match, Ken Venturi handled the post-match interview. He asked me what I thought. I simply told him, "Ken, I don't know if Joe Dey knows it or not, but some of those guys out there may be taking pills. Maybe he should give golfers saliva tests like they do race horses?"

This was probably passed over by all who heard it as just another joke by Tommy Bolt. I probably said it in a half-joking manner at the time. But the truth is, many professional golfers today do take pills. They take all kinds of pills.

Not too long ago, I was visiting with a couple of touring friends in a motel room. On their dresser was a row of pill bottles as long as a three-wood. I have never seen so many bottles. They had pills to go to sleep with, to get up with, to tee off with, to take after nine holes, and to take after eighteen holes. As I stood there shaking each little bottle, I told the players, "You guys won't live to be fifty-five years old. Nobody will ever have to worry about you boys being senior champions." One of them told me he didn't expect to live to be fifty.

Last summer, at one of the big tournaments up North, I was walking out of the locker room when I saw one of the named pros who had paused by the drinking fountain. He opened a bottle and popped a great big white pill in his mouth. "What in the hell was that?" I asked him. "It is as big as a golf ball."

He smiled and said, "It's for gout." I didn't believe it. I told

81

him so. "Gout my goofus. As nervous as you are, you have to be taking something to get you around nine holes."

I don't think I would be justified in preaching so hard against these pills if I didn't have some sort of answer to the problem. I can easily see how players feel they need something to maintain the monotonous pace of tour golf. The travel alone takes a lot out of a man. I have tried everything. I mean when I talk about the fellows of years ago who used to seek relaxation from whiskey bottles, I, too, had my share of the pinch bottle. As I said, I, too, have tried tranquilizers.

Whiskey, I might point out, is not the relaxer the golfer needs. He cannot be sure how he will feel the next morning. And the next round is the most important one a golfer ever plays. Tranquilizers do nothing for the player. They hinder coordination.

So, what can the player do?

Well, I can only tell you that I played the best golf of my life at Southern Hills, Tulsa, in 1958. That was the weekend I won the National Open. That weekend, I had a few drinks. Maybe one or two a night before my dinner. I didn't even take an aspirin that week. The answer, as I look back on it, was peace of mind. I was a happy man going into the tournament. I had no outside worries. I went there to play the National Open and that was all I had on my mind the entire week. This took preparation. I got all my affairs straight before I went to the tournament. I resigned from the world, except for that particular tournament. It's really strange as I look back on it, but I knew the moment I hit that first shot that I was going to win the Open. That's how free my mind was.

It is my contention that a man can get the maximum output from his mind and body if he applies both in the same direction. Nature sees to that. He does not have to use a stimulant, nor does he have to use a relaxant.

Unlike football and baseball, the PGA has no rules against its players using pills. But man himself, especially the professional golfer, should set up his own rules. Pep pills, tranquilizers, and the like are not good things for anybody. And it is my firm conviction that the man who relies on them is killing himself fast. All those players today who take pills on tour may be getting along well despite them. But I was out there first when whiskey was the way. The bottle sent a ton of them home early. Soon, the pillbox has got to start taking its toll.

There's only one real way to play professional golf. That's to have a clear mind. Be happy, free of absolutely any worries at all. That, besides holing a jillion putts every day, is the only way I know to be a golf champion.

What would you say was Tommy Bolt's one big weakness?

You can bet both cheeks it is not throwing golf clubs, not breaking golf clubs, and not throwing caddies.

I have a short fuse, sure. Something happens I don't like and right now I'm hot about it. I scream to high heaven. I know I'm right about it and I confront the head man. I wouldn't think of chewing out an elevator operator because I didn't like something about the building. I'd go to the owner of the building if I could find him. If not, I'd go to the superintendent.

It's the same in golf. If I heard the guys crying among themselves about something which I, too, thought was wrong, I'd go to the top man on hand. The other guys couldn't do anything about the problem anyhow. I'd go right to the top. It wouldn't take me long to get hot along with the rest of them if nothing was done about the particular situation. I'm beginning to see now, though, why I was always the one they came to when something needed to be brought out in the open.

Perhaps my biggest weakness was the one I failed to see. It often happens like that. They knew that if I went to battle over

83

some issue then I would wind up getting mad at everybody in sight and that it would take its toll on my golf game. They could just forget about Old Tom winning the golf tournament for that week, or even making much money.

So, to answer point-blank, my biggest weakness was the temper, 30 percent, and the fact that I would always fight another guy's battle, 70 percent.

Why, over in Hawaii a few years ago, Billy Casper launched a golf club in the Pacific Ocean. I didn't see it. I wasn't anywhere around that part of the course. But I hadn't been off the course twenty minutes when guys who had seen Casper heave that jessie were bugging me about it. Now, how do you like that? They wanted him reported and they didn't want to do it themselves. They knew I would. I used to get all the reports like that. If anybody threw a golf club, I was the man to do the squealing. But this Casper thing was different. Everybody who saw him trying to fish that thing out of the ocean came to me and told me about it. Half the field wanted him reported. What does that say for Mr. Casper's popularity among the players?

I went straight to the officials. It cost him $100, just as it has always cost me.

It was something like this that Bob Rosburg did to me in 1969 that cost me a golf tournament and allowed Rosburg, the agitator, to win the top money.

We were playing in the National Club Pro Championship in Arizona. Rosburg instigated a big fight over the caddies and then forgot all about it, put that little grin on his face all week, and paid attention to his golf game. Me? I was still fighting the officials for the first two rounds and was dropping five shots behind. I closed down on him at the end and would have caught him if we had had four more holes.

Here's what happened.

The PGA officials running the tournament announced that all caddies would be drawn from a hat. No one could select his own caddie. Well, this would have been okay with most people, if the officials had done it early enough. But they waited until most of us had caddies. I had gotten out there early. So had Rosburg. We both had picked our own caddies. I had played three practice rounds with my boy. He was a college boy who played on the golf team, but I didn't know in advance he was good. I was set to go, when suddenly, out of a clear blue sky, the officials said we couldn't use those boys. We'd have to draw others. It seems that some of the home pros there had complained that we had the best of it with our caddies.

Our past tour experience gave us the best of it anyway when we showed up to play. The caddie wasn't going to make any difference in what I did to them on the golf course. I told them they couldn't beat me if they had Palmer or Nicklaus caddying for them.

Rosburg was the leader against the officials. He was red-faced and steaming. You could see those glasses fogging up. Also, there was Mike Souchak and George Bayer on our side. We were the biggest names in the tournament. We decided to tell them we weren't going to play. We'd just withdraw if they took our caddies away from us.

Well, that's as far as the "we" part of it went. When the going really got hot, it was just me doing the fighting. Joe Black was running the tournament and I challenged him right quick. I looked over my shoulder for some support and there wasn't anybody around. There was Rosburg grinning like a jackass eating briars.

It went on for two days. I was thinking about calling Joe Dey. I even thought about taking it to the Supreme Court. When the smoke cleared, Souchak and Bayer didn't qualify. Rosburg, the first one to gripe, won the tournament. And the man who carried on the fight, Old Dad, shot 70-72-68-69.

Boy, it took me six weeks to get over that. Hell, I may not be over it yet. I told Rosburg what I thought of him before he got out of there.

And I guess some of those home club pros know how I feel too.

They said, "It ain't fair. Bolt has a professional caddie. The kid's the best player at the school out there." What the hell did I know? All I did was go to the course and pick out a boy I thought looked as if he knew what was going on. I'm not trying to flaunt anything over anybody, but I am a name player. I play well. And I'm not the easiest man in the world to caddie for.

When they finally did make us draw, I fired the one they made me take because he had never been on a course before. I told him I'd see him later.

You mean to tell me that the PGA doesn't think we should be privileged to select our own caddie? A guy starts wondering what he worked all those years for. He wonders that after he finishes wondering if all those PGA people have to worry about is who is going to do the caddying?

Why has the Masters Championship been criticized so in recent years?

Simply because it deserved it.

There is not one golfer in the world who can honestly say that the Masters is a major championship. It is not major simply because the people who run it apparently do not wish to make it a major championship. Honestly, I can't tell you how the Masters has gained the status it has. They squirmed it in with the National Open and the PGA Championship somehow. The British Open is the fourth tournament considered among the big four major championships. I'll say this about the British Open, it has become better in recent years. But still you can't compare it with the United States National Open, the biggest of them all, and the PGA Championship. However, I will say that today the British Open is just as big as the Masters.

In being so selective with the United States tour invitees, the

Masters committee has caused considerable friction among the players. But here again we have a problem that the PGA or the Tournament Players Division refuses to act upon. They stand idly by while this committee makes people angry. It is hard for any member of the PGA to understand how one tournament can carry that much weight. Also, by refusing to accept the outstanding young and old players on tour who might win the tournament, the Masters indicates to me that it does not want to become a major championship.

The Masters committee sets up its own regulations as to who is eligible for its tournament. It invites players to this country who otherwise wouldn't be eligible for our tour events unless they qualified as our boys have to do. Also, they pour in an overwhelming number of amateur players.

It was just last summer that the Masters Committee finally gave enough to permit winners on our PGA tour to be eligible. This is a concession almost forced on them by some honest writers.

Please, don't think I'm knocking the idea of outstanding amateurs competing with tournament professionals. This may well be good. But I do not think it is a good idea for amateurs to compete in big tournaments when they are taking up room that might go to professionals who could get a chance at the money. This defeats the very objective of the PGA as the players see the association.

Remember when Lee Trevino walked away from the Masters and said he'd never go back? Well, Lee passed it off simply. He said he hit the ball too low to play Augusta. If you have seen Lee Trevino play golf, you know he plays well enough to play golf anywhere. What probably happened is that when Lee went there after winning the National Open Championship at Rochester, he was treated as if he were a caddie. They can do that there. They have little regard for the feelings of anybody, save a few special players who write them nice letters after the tournament is over telling them what a delightful show they put on.

Most of the touring pros will tell you that each year we play many, many tournaments far tougher than the Masters. I've heard them say , "What's the Masters? Every time we tee it up for a hundred and fifty thousand dollars we are playing against a tougher field than they have at Augusta." This is true simply because the Masters committee has its set of little rules that go dead against the grain of the PGA. But no one does anything about it. Who in the world are they afraid of?

One peculiar way they had of permitting a player to enter the event was to take a vote of former champions. These players could propose any golfer not otherwise eligible for the event. I know that in 1970 I got considerable votes from my friends who had won the tournament. But Bob Murphy got the invitation. He was already invited. Who counted those votes, I wonder? Someone who'd rather have Bob Murphy playing up there than Tommy Bolt. And what he wants is okay with me. I have no respect for anyone who is doing professional golf an injustice, knows it, and refuses to bend in any way to cut down on the friction he is causing between an association and its members.

By permitting the Masters to be so choosy in who can play there, the PGA and the Tournament Players Division are letting the committee jumble up many things. Each year around Labor Day, they have a World Series of Golf. This is for big money, $75,000. They take the winners of the Masters, British Open, National Open, and PGA—four men in all.

Okay, think right quick how many young players the Masters eliminates immediately. They say who is to play at Augusta. That means they are saying who will have three chances and who will have four chances to play in the World Series of Golf.

Then there is the British Open. The prize money isn't high there. It's mainly a prestige thing. You'll find most of the American golfers playing there are players who have made it in this country, and are looking for prestige rather than money. That eliminates still more of the hard-working crowd. So, in effect, the average young touring player, the kid who certainly

88

needs the money, has only two chances to play in the World Series of Golf, while the big-name fellows, the fellows who have made it, have four shots.

There was a time when I thought that the players themselves would rebel, boycott the Masters, and right this wrong that is being done all players. Most of those players on top now remember the days when they were forced to sit out the Masters. They know how unfair it seemed to them then. I'll bet a lot of them vowed that someday, if they got the chance, they would do something about it. Well, some of them got the chance. What did they do? They waited until their time came and then figured they'd let the rest of the players get there the best way they could.

Trevino won't be the last player to pull away, swearing he'll never go back. There will be more who'll probably do the same thing on conscience alone. Or should do it. The only thing the Masters has that many of the other and better tournaments do not have is prestige. How they got it, I'm not really sure. It has always puzzled me how they squeezed that event in as a major championship.

Can golf professionals cheat?

They can and they have.

One thing about cheating in professional golf, it is like murder. You are not a murderer unless you are convicted of it in court. Same way in golf, guys may be cheating out there every day, but unless they are caught and suspended, they are not cheaters in the eyes of the PGA.

Some of the fellows I have seen and played with over the last twenty-five years could not be termed cheaters simply because they were never caught and convicted. But I remember them. I know who they are. You learn to know who will take advantage of particular situations and who will not. When you are paired with some cat who is inclined to take advantage of a situation, then you pay a little more attention to what he is doing and a little less to what you are supposed to do. It makes for an unhappy round usually.

It never ceases to amaze me when I see a good golf player, one who is admired by the public, take advantage of a rule of golf, or just do some outright cheating. One thing about it, golf rules are written so that if you see a fellow player cheat and you do not report it, you are guilty of cheating yourself. So, before I go one step further, let me make it clear that some of them are so good at it that you can't be sure, can't be sure enough to involve yourself in an argument that will doubtless end up before the rules committee in a your-word-against-his-word debate.

Some of the methods of cheating are so subtle and so ingenious that it makes a guy suspect that if these players thought as much about their swings as they did about taking advantage of the rules they wouldn't have to cheat.

Try this one. The rules of the game say you cannot bend or break anything to improve your lie. But how about those guys who hit the ball in four- to six-inch rough. The cheaters will stand over the ball a long time. They look like actors in a movie with that final shot to win the National Open championship. If the hole is long enough, they will first pull out a wood. They take their stance, place the club behind the ball, stand there a long, long time. Well, if you are standing out in the fairway, maybe fifty yards away, it is impossible to tell how hard they are pressing down behind that ball. But believe me, they are pressing hard, harder than they are supposed to, for when they finally hit the shot they have put the wood club back in the bag, drawn an iron, and sent that jessie flying out of those weeds as if they had it on a tee.

Clayton Heafner was a stickler for the rules. Years ago, he was paired with a player who on several occasions hit drives in the rough. Every time he pulled a wood, stood over the ball a while, then returned to his bag for an iron. Ole Clayt knew what was going on. The next time the player got a bit more bold. It wasn't a long hole. A wood was far too much club. Clayt saw him pull it out and walk to his ball. He yelled: "Okay, you have made your choice now. I want to see you hit it. If you change clubs this time you and I have a meeting with the rules committee." The poor guy had to stand there with a three-wood and smack that ball out of six-inch grass to a green no more than 160 yards away. It resulted in a topped shot and a double bogey six. Heafner had served as his own rules committee in that case.

Another time we were playing the St. Petersburg Open at the Pasadena Golf Club. It had rained all week and on Friday the rules committee permitted us to improve our lies all over the course. Actually, this is a football game. You look around and see the ball in a guy's hand, more than you see it on the ground. You have to watch them carefully here; many of them will walk it toward the hole. All the improved-lie rule means is that the player can lift his ball, clean it, and replace it, NO NEARER THE HOLE, a set distance from its original position.

The eighteenth hole at Pasadena is a par five. They tell the story of the player who hit a reasonably good drive out in the fairway. He walked down to his ball and for some unknown reason started ranting and raving to high heaven. He was beating his driver in the ground. His playing partners were on the other side of the fairway. They had no idea what was going on. When it came time to hit, the player who apparently was so upset sent a low, zooming shot into the green not more than fifteen feet from the cup. He had a sure birdie and reasonably easy eagle putt. What had happened, his partners soon knew, was that he wasn't mad at all when he walked to his ball. He knew that not many players were going to be able to reach that eighteenth hole in two. It was wet, the ball wouldn't roll. He pretended to be upset, banged his driver in the ground, raised himself about a two-inch chunk of wet turf, and used that for a tee. He lifted his ball, cleaned it, placed it on that turf and owned as pretty a driver lie as you have ever seen.

You are allowed to pick up loose impediments behind your ball in the fairway or rough. This means pieces of paper, leaves or branches, and such as that. But when you hit the ball into sandy rough, you are not allowed to pick up pebbles or sand. I've seen them lean over that thing in sandy rough, pretend to be picking up loose impediments and quickly brush a finger behind the ball. All this does is take away about a quarter-inch of sand, leaving the ball teed high and dry for any shot they want to hit. I have to laugh when I see these kids out there doing that now. I saw players doing it twenty-five years ago. I tell myself, "Well, as many changes as we have had in twenty-five years, everything has stayed pretty much the same."

I've seen them walk in sand traps, not settle on the club they carried with them, and walk out to get another one. But on the way out, or back in the second time, they stepped behind their ball and gave themselves a beautiful lie, beautiful compared to the one they owned when they rolled into the bunker. One with all that sand piled behind the ball.

You meet all kinds of people playing golf. I would say that the majority were okay guys. The kind of guys who are willing to take the good with the bad and the kind of guys you enjoy associating with. But you meet the other kind, too. The kind who think they are never supposed to hit a ball out of bounds, never supposed to get a bad break and, if they didn't have company out there, never would get a bad break. But the fellow who really gets under my skin—and I'm quick to tell him so—is the fellow who seems anxious for you to break or bend a rule. He operates on the theory, "I'll do you a favor now, you can repay sometime later in the round." This is the kind of fellow I love to see suffer out there. It is hard to birddog a playing partner and play your own game. But once I catch some guy out there trying to do me favors, I'll just trot along behind him a while and watch him carefully on every shot. He soon knows what I'm doing. And he had better get a good grip on his concentration.

I always admired Skip Alexander for a story someone told me about him. Years ago Skip was a fine touring professional. His career was interrupted by a horrible airplane crash, but Skip came out of it to continue playing some golf. He is now located in St. Petersburg, Florida, as pro at the Lakewood Country Club course. Once, competing in the Florida Open Championship at Port St. Lucie, Skip was playing the ninth hole. He had hit his second shot into trees at this par fiver. There had been some delay. Skip and his partners had trouble locating the ball. Finally, one of his playing partners found the ball and Skip played a fine iron shot through the branches onto the back edge of the green.

"Fine shot," said the playing partner, who had stood there and watched Skip hit.

"It's okay," said Skip, "but I lie four."

"What do you mean four?" asked the other player. "That was your third."

"No," said Skip. "The ball moved as I addressed it."

"It didn't move," said the player. "I didn't see it."

"God saw it move," said Skip.

This was a great thing for Alexander to say to the man who obviously wanted Skip to know that he was willing to forget what had happened in the woods. You can bet that somewhere on the back nine, if that player had needed relief, he would have called on Skip to repay the favor he had done him on the ninth hole. But it wasn't working with Skip. He took his hardships, and those playing with him had better be ready to take theirs.

Golf needs more men like that. Golf is a gentleman's game, they say. But you sure can find a lot of gentlemen out there willing to cheat to keep that bogey off the score card.

What about the Golden One—the Bear—Jack Nicklaus?

Remember the movie *The Cincinnati Kid?*

Well, that fellow was a poker player. But the Columbus Kid is a

93

golf player. And unlike the poker player from Cincy, the Columbus Kid isn't going to bow to anyone. Jack Nicklaus is the best golf player in the world today and has been for ten years. Why, Palmer was voted the Athlete of the Decade late in 1969. But for most of that very decade he spent his time, just like the rest of us, trying to figure a way to bring Jack down on the golf course. And just like the rest of us he failed to figure it out.

Remember back three, four years ago when Snead said that Nicklaus would be burned out by the time he was thirty years old? Well, Jack's thirty now and you could get Snead to part with some of that money he has buried away if Jack so much as suggested he needed a partner for the next ten years. Sam would pay his expenses just for half the winnings. Instead of being burned out, Jack has burned out a lot of other players.

I always compare what Nicklaus has done in golf to what Roger Maris did in baseball. Back in 1961 when Roger smacked sixty-one home runs, people weren't ready to accept it. They screamed he played more games than Babe Ruth. They claimed that Roger wasn't deserving to move to the head of the list as the greatest hitter of home runs for one season. Maris, being one heck of a nice guy, accepted this and philosophically told himself that he must pay the penalty for outdoing a national idol. "I was fighting a ghost," he said, "and there wasn't any way I could win the battle."

Well, it wasn't that Nicklaus was fighting a man who couldn't defend himself. Palmer was there and trying all he could to stop Jack's relentless march to the top. But just the same, Arnie was the king in the public's eye and Jack became the villain simply because he dared to outplay "the Man."

But Jack took on Palmer. He took on his army and proved to all the people who know golf—especially the players—that he was the better man. I know one thing, it had to be tough for Jack during those rounds when he was paired with Palmer. People absolutely pulled for Arnie and against him. That would demoralize most players. It would have killed me. But Jack is made of something different. It seemed to make him more determined.

94

Odd thing about it all is that Jack is a super person. If the public took time to know Jack, it would accept him every bit as quickly as it did Palmer. Somehow the public got the idea that Jack always had money. He was portrayed as the rich, babyish kid, sort of spoiled, who had had things handed to him all his life. This is not true. Jack, fortunately, never had to worry about meals and such, but believe me, he put as much time in building his golf game as Palmer did. And he must have done a better job of it, for he wasn't as long getting to the meat of the thing as Palmer was.

In my mind the best thing that ever happened to Nicklaus and the worst thing that happened to the rest of those players out there is when Jack cut his strings with Mark McCormack during the 1970 season. McCormack is the attorney who took over Palmer and made him image-wise throughout the world. There was a lot of talk going around that Jack was getting the worst of this deal. Here he was the best man by far on the golf course and the Number Two man in the McCormack stable. Just as it was no contest when the two—Palmer and Nicklaus—were playing on a golf course (it was all Nicklaus), it was also no contest between them when McCormack was building their images. Palmer was getting all the gravy. Now if McCormack comes back with, "I did as much for Jack as I did for Arnie," then write down one winner and one failure for Mr. McCormack. And also ask him why Jack didn't stay around for all those favors he was doing him.

You've never seen a happier fellow than Nicklaus since he left McCormack. And you've never seen a golfer playing better. It may turn out to be the worst thing that ever happened to McCormack and the best thing that ever happened to Jack Nicklaus. This man is a money machine. He is by far the most valuable piece of athletic merchandise in the world today. And when you compare him to other sports figures, don't stop with top athletes, think in terms of franchise. Don't be surprised if in five years you hear Mark McCormack say, "You know I had that guy for a while. It was a mistake letting him get away." Good for

95

Jack getting away. He needed Mark McCormack like he needed a busted wrist.

By now you must have the idea I think Jack Nicklaus can play a little, huh. Well, why is he the best player in the world? One big reason is that he has learned to hit the ball straight. The kid from Columbus hits it oh-high-oh and oh-far-oh and oh-straight-oh. Those sand bunkers they put out in those fairways aren't put there for him. They are there to bedevil the rest of us. Jack just tees his little whitey high and flies it out over those sand traps. It's good-bye and where's my eight-iron?

As you pass through these pages you will notice that I stress the importance of concentration in golf. Well, just imagine what Jack has lived with. He has been the best player in the game for years now and few people want to accept it. I don't know what he has to do to prove it to the rest of them. He must be thinking the same thing. But this doesn't bother him. He applies his mind to what he must do with those clubs and he does the job. If you need further proof that he is the king of concentration, then remember that he was the guy who came along and took Arnie and Arnie's Army and sent them into a hasty retreat on golf courses all over the world.

If I were looking at golf through the eyes of the Golden Bear, I wouldn't be thinking Big Three! I would be thinking Big Me! Because Jack Nicklaus is king of the roost. And, Snead, he's just thirty years old!

How tough is it to make your living gambling at golf?

You need more equipment to be a successful gambler than you do to play the tour. To gamble, you have to be 50 percent actor and 50 percent golfer. You have to steal a cat's money and make him love it. The ideal thing, the thing all pro golfers look for are

96

the celebrity nuts. There are guys who just like to play golf with professionals. Most of these players have a few bucks and don't mind paying that ten or twenty dollars Nassau just to be in the company of the pro. I call these guys "associates." They are trying to hypo their ego. Whenever I go to a tournament and some player asks if I have a foursome for a practice round, I'll smile, wink, and say, "Not today, I have me a couple of associates coming out." They get the message.

To the golf professional a game such as this is nothing but an out-and-out stickup. It is simply done with golf clubs and not a mask and gun. The pro's conscience does not figure in here because he has long ago told himself that he is one of the stars of the game and that any amateur wishing to play with him should pay the fee. Is this any worse than a man wanting legal advice paying a lawyer or a man needing medical advice paying a doctor?

Now a touring professional can get away with this. He's here today, 500 miles down the road tomorrow. But many of the club professionals see how easily this is done by the touring pros and they try it. First thing you know, the club pro is here today, 500 miles down the road the next day, and they hadn't planned to travel. I only know one thing that will get a home pro fired quicker than gambling with his male members on the golf course. The other thing is hustling his male members' wives off the golf course.

Think what a trap the home pro has himself in when he gambles, whether he loses or wins big money. He can't afford a lot of losing—he isn't making the kind of money most of his members are if he has a job at a big country club. But he can't afford to keep winning either; there's a deep pride in most golfers, and if they continually lose their money to one person, then they feel as if this person is cheating them, not coming up with enough strokes to make it a fair game. As soon as enough members get this idea about the home professional, he can start packing the old buggy. He's a free agent again.

I only dropped one of my twenty-five years being a club pro. The rest I spent on tour, doing exactly as Old Tom wanted to do. Why, even when I bought the Golden Tee course in Sarasota, I hired a club pro. I didn't want the job. The year I spent at the Knollwood Country Club in Los Angeles was enough for me. There's an area where most members have plenty of cash. Knollwood was a growing club and one of my jobs was to play around the various clubs in town and try to secure more members for Knollwood.

My club already had some of the biggies, Milton Berle, Jeff Chandler, Bob Hope, and Dean Martin. Dean and I played almost every day. Deano would show up at the bar every morning. He would hoist a couple of martinis and we'd bat that ball around all afternoon. He owned a nine handicap in those days. It was one of those proud nines. He couldn't play to it. He could pay to it, though. He is a great guy, and knowing and playing with him in those days is one of the few bright spots I recall of my year (1957) at Knollwood.

I had me a one-year contract with those people. I hadn't served many months of it before I knew I was going to wave them good-bye when that first year ended. I feel I did most of the things that are expected of a home pro. I kept a well-stocked, attractive pro shop. There was no squawk there. I gave the lessons that were expected of me. I bowed to the big shots and went out of my way to please the big shots' wives.

BUT, I played a lot of golf. Playing golf has always been my business. I hadn't planned to retire as a player when I signed that one-year contract. I think the feeling among the members who were anti-Bolt was that I should bury any ideas I had of rejoining the tour and be content keeping the scoreboard on ladies day, teaching the fat guys to break 80, and putting new grips on golf clubs they had bought somewhere else. This wasn't for Old Dad, pardner.

I don't know how happy some of those members were when I left, but they can multiply it by 1,000 and know how happy I was.

If I hadn't won the National Open the next summer, I probably would mark down leaving that club job as the happiest moment of my life. So much for scuffling with club members, club jobs, and tying yourself to 400 frustrated cats and their frustrated wives, swings and demands.

When I first started playing golf, I had the incentive to play well and play for my cash. I wanted to quit the construction job for good. It isn't hard to understand, however, that the streets are not crawling with guys willing to give you their money on the golf course. I learned early not to take just any golf game and hope I made money. I learned patience. Wait on that live mullet to come along and maybe it would make up for all those fruitless days you spent on the practice tee. In the meantime, I was winning amateur tournaments and collecting merchandise prizes. I would sell these things and that kept me going until I could find another mullet or two.

You don't gamble at golf long before you find that a good part of it is done before anybody ever strikes at the first golf ball. Everybody, even some of the mullet, wants the best of it off the first tee. They used to ask me which was the most important hole in golf. I'd answer, "The most important hole in golf is not a hole at all, it is a tee. The first tee." If you can make comfortable contracts on the first tee, you don't have to go near a practice tee the rest of your life.

When we were gambling with our mullet, we had names for them. A real good first-tee man was called an "arranger." If he felt he needed three strokes a side to break even, he'd start by asking for five and taking four. I hadn't been at it long before I became a pretty good "arranger" myself.

There is a story about the wealthy guy in town who died suddenly. When his attorney produced the will, there was nothing there but a note. It read:

"No doubt you relatives will be surprised to find that I have no money to leave you. You all know that I worked hard all my life, and if I had one vice it was nothing more than gambling on the golf course. May I explain to you now that this is perhaps the worst of all the vices. But I want you to all know that I went to my just reward a happy man. I believe in the end that I cured my hook to a point that I was an honest five-handicap golf player. There weren't more than six players in the entire club that I could not have beaten even. I died a happy man. Knowing this, and forgiving me for not leaving any money, I know that you will meet my last request. I would like my body cut into eighteen pieces. I would like one piece buried ceremoniously on each of the country club's holes. I then would rest in peace near the game I so dearly loved."

The lawyer thought he was through. Then a separate piece of paper fell to the table. He picked it up and read:

"Oh, yes, and bury my ass on the first tee. That is where I lost it."

This is one of the things a guy "on the hustle" has to be leery of when he is trying to make ends meet with his golf clubs. He doesn't want to get so anxious to win money that he gives his cash away on the first tee. But he also should be able to recognize those mullet who can't resist making the bad game just to have a game.

Someone once told me, "Tommy, the second best thing in the world is betting and losing. The worst thing is not betting at all. The idea is to have the action." I never went for that one. But I owned me a bunch of cats that I thought felt that way. And I was forever looking for them.

During the years I was working at the construction job and playing golf when I had time, word drifted over to Texas that there was some pretty good action at Hot Springs, Arkansas. This interested me when I heard it, but there wasn't anything I could do about it. I filed it away for a rainy day.

Hot Springs was a big-time resort area. Gibby Sellers was the pro there. Years later, when I got to know Gibby real well, he told me that, in the early days, Al Capone's crowd would visit Hot

Springs. "They loved to play golf," said Gibby. "They didn't care what the tariff was. Nearly all of them played golf and they brought their money wrapped in bailing wire."

Gibby would be telling me this and he'd see me licking my lips. He'd go on, "There they went, down that first fairway. The players in the middle of the fairway with their caddies and on either side, walking along the rough, would be other 'caddies' carrying bags without clubs in them. Nothing at all sticking out of the bags."

I asked Gibby, "What the hell was that all about?"

Gibby said, "Well, tucked neatly in those bags were tommy guns. This was sort of protection against any outside interference. And, too, often guys from different gangs would be playing against each other and it was simply to see that everybody played the game as the rules suggested they should. It was about as honest a golf game as you would ever want to watch."

"I can appreciate that," I said.

I used to love to hear Gibby tell those stories. They intrigued me. I often wondered what it would be like to putt for thousands of dollars knowing that over there in the woods a man was standing with a tommy gun in case there was some misunderstanding about the rules. Now that's a good way to firm up the backswing. Or maybe shorten up the backswing.

As I said, I had just heard of Hot Springs when I was a carpenter in Houston. I didn't know Sellers then. I heard that rich guys with bad swings hung around there. These guys came to Hot Springs to take baths in the mineral waters, and many of them were taking baths on the golf course, too.

Memorial Park in Houston was a good place to find action. A lot of golfers hung around there, and most of them weren't afraid to bet their cash. I remember one guy telling me, "I brought it out here to bet it. Money won't grow in your pocket." Golf hustlers have a way of making money sound so insignificant. That is what I meant about being 50 percent actor. You have to entice mullet to play with you by talking down the money. I used to play with a guy who'd pay off and say, "Here's the money. It's not anything but a better grade of toilet paper."

It was easy to weed out the guys we didn't want to play with. We'd look for guys who loved their money too much. They weren't good mullet. They'd play maybe one time, feeling out the game. They would start by betting $2 at most. If they lost, they weren't hurt for their free look and they had a ball playing with good players. We'd try to get the ante higher than $2. If they were just peeping to see how the battle went, we wanted to leave a scar at least.

And then there were times when the good gambler had to be a good nurse. It was bad at times to belt a mullet's head off the first time out. Funny thing, some guys don't figure good. They can't get the economic soundness of losing $100 once and heading for the hills against losing $20 ten times. It was a poor gambler who would beat a new mullet for that fast $100 when he could have kept the guy interested for two weeks and won $20 each day. That's what I mean when I say it takes patience.

I used to wonder a bit about Hogan on tour. Who in the world would have gone out there and played Ben Hogan a $100 Nassau? It was unthinkable. But Ben liked a little action. He was clever. On days before the tournament started we'd get a foursome and play a game called "type shots." As I think back on it, it was a game made for Hogan. We'd never count putts at all. We'd play $1 for a ball in the fairway and $1 for a ball on the green closest to the hole. The putts didn't mean a thing. Well, you can imagine what this was for Hogan. He had three guys playing him eighteen holes and betting him $2 per hole each. I don't remember eating any meals at night that Ben paid for.

In Houston, I played a lot of golf with Sid Mueller. He had a hair-restoring business. It had to be a good business because Sid would show up at the course with all his pockets bulging with cash. Sid was honest about his golf gambling. He knew I could beat him. But he played and paid without ever opening his mouth. I liked him and respected his ability. I gave him fair bets. But when time came to pay, there he was digging in one of those pockets. One time there he handed me $800 and told me to take off for the tour and see how far I could go. He didn't expect anything in return. He wanted me to try my hand with the world's greatest gamblers.

It was during this time that I went to Springfield, Missouri, for a small $5,000 tournament. I made a little money there and was in no particular hurry to go back to Houston. I remember talking to a bunch of guys I was traveling with and deciding to give Hot Springs a shot.

We weren't in Hot Springs two days before someone introduced us to a rich furniture manufacturer from Little Rock. He'd come to Hot Springs to take the cure. They told me he'd get drunk, soak it out in the baths, and take off to the golf course with another fifth of whiskey in his golf bag. I met him and a game was arranged. He talked some big money. His first bet was a $1,000 Nassau.

There were five of us traveling together and we had to pool our money to put up. I was selected to do the playing. I had to spot the guy half a stroke a hole. I won easy the first day, and he said he wanted one more dose of it the next day. He also said that we would have to come up with some more shots. Next time we teed off he got a full shot on some holes and half a shot on the rest of them.

The whole thing boiled down to the sixteenth hole that last day. I remember it was a stroke hole and I had knocked in a birdie. He was left out there on the green with a six-foot putt for his birdie. If he made it he won the hole and would go one-up on the match with half strokes at the last two holes.

He went way over to the corner of the green and took ten or twenty practice putts. I'll never forget it. He talked to himself, "Now come on. You know you can make this putt. Calm down now. You know what this putt means to you." Then he would walk back over to his putt and look at it a long time. He was taking so long with the thing that I was getting nervous. Can you imagine what that money meant to us in those days? We had figured it out, if he missed his putt we would win $7,500 for the two days.

Finally, he bent over his putt and just stood there. He didn't move for the longest time. Then, all of a sudden, as if someone had sent a bolt of electricity up the putter and shocked him, he threw his putter straight out away from him in a twirling motion. He picked up his ball, yelled, "I can't hit it. I can't hit it," and walked to the next tee. Never in my life have I seen "the Thing" grab a man the way it did him.

I found out something about "the Thing" that day. If you can keep it away from you and let it grab the other guy, then you could have yourself a pretty good partner. That furniture man was attacked so suddenly and fiercely by whatever it is that attacks golfers that I looked around in the trees to see if there was some more coming after me. Since then, I've held a mortal fear of "the Thing." I've tried to fight it off with intense concentration. I've seen players choke out there right down to their navels. It's a pitiful sight.

This is another thing that golf gamblers look for in a man. How subject is that particular golfer to choking? The word used to leak in a hurry when someone found a mullet who could play like hell for $10 or $20, but jack that ante up to $50 and $100 and he'd walk those fairways hand in hand with "the Thing." We used to refer to this as "stacking it (the money) right up to his chin." Let him see it. Let him get a good smell of what we were playing for. Give "the Thing" a good reason to swoop.

These methods were only good for gamblers who were going to hang around a particular course and have time to feel out the players. Few of them did us any good when we went on tour. We weren't in the same town very long. What we had to depend on was the actual fact we were pros and that we could play better than any of the local talent that might come along. And it did come along.

Most of my little games of chance came during my early days on tour when I wasn't making the cut every week. When we'd miss one town, we'd head on down the road. Head to that next tournament. When we got there, we'd start the search. We'd look for the best of the amateur players and hope he had money or had someone who wanted to back him with their cash. It would usually work, too. There always seemed to be someone who could swing the club pretty well and someone who thought he could beat us. What helped us was the fact that we hadn't made the cut in the last tournament. These local people didn't think we could play at all. They didn't realize how tough it was out there. They didn't know that some pretty good players missed that cut every week.

The object of the games in those days was to find some sucker who would be good for the caddie fee, the room rent, and maybe the gasoline money. You know, those incidentals that the PGA expected you to pay so that you could be one of their stars. I found that tour players would much rather find someone away from the tour life to gamble with than pick on each other. There was some gambling among the players themselves, but not much. Not as much as there was between the players and some outsider who had one of those miracle kids who thought he could beat the pros on his home course. I wonder how many of those guys are in the poorhouses across the country today?

Is golf a good profession for a youngster to follow?

Not my youngster. I'd rather see him pursue medicine, or law.

Golf was good to me. But no one did me any early favors. I didn't find any shortcuts. Tour golf is to men what hide-and-seek is to youngsters. Except the men are paying their cash to play the game. When one of those tournaments starts, all who aren't ready can't hide over.

There are thousands of young boys over the country who win little junior tournaments and their daddys will get all excited about the prospects of raising another Snead or Hogan or Palmer. Man, that boy is going to have to have more than a junior trophy to ever even get a player's card to prove he might be a Snead, Hogan, or Palmer. It costs $25,000 or $30,000 a year just to be where the action is, 75 percent of the time. If you are going to play every tournament they have, then you'll spend more than that showing up.

When I think back on the fine golfers who have tried the tour and failed, I realize how important it is to have so many other things besides an ability to hit the golf ball. There are a bunch of rabbits out there who can hit that thing as good as the guy who wins on Sunday. But there's always that something that's missing.

Seems to me it was Frank Beard who said, three or four years ago, "A lot of mothers are going to get mad at me. But if you are thinking of sending your son out on tour, you'd better get used to him gambling his allowance away on the golf course when he's a youngster."

There are not many golf champions who don't know what Frank was talking about. In order for a man to win at this thing, and, mind you, there have been exceptions, he is better off if he has some "hustle" in him. Now don't confuse this "hustle" with what they say baseball and football players have. I mean "hustle" like gambling instinct. I mean you'd better have the kind of boy who can bet his cheese on his golf game and beat every kid in the block. This will probably cause the Tournament Players Division Director, Joe Dey, to hide his head, but Mr. Dey had better understand right now that he is in charge of some guys who have done plenty of hustling in their day. Most of your boys, Mr. Dey, will bet their cash.

What I think is hurting golf today and making it unattractive for youngsters are the backers. Yeah, I know, I had a couple. But in those days, the backers I had were trying to help me. They weren't putting up money hoping I would make them rich. Today, the majority of the backers and agents aren't trying to help anybody. They're trying to make money. Professional golf probably hasn't realized it yet, but it is in business with all types of people. Every time a kid gets his player's card and backing, professional golf has a new partner.

It was Tony Lema, I think, who found some friends to back him. For years Tony struggled out there. But he worked hard for those guys. Then when Tony got so he could make something of himself, the backers didn't want to permit him to buy up his contract. How fair was that for the guy who did the work?

Most of the big-time backers of today aren't trying to help some deserving kid who worked hard perfecting a good golf swing. Those backers are trying to get rich with those big purses. And the kid is so desperate to get out there and try that he signs almost anything for the chance.

This isn't nearly all of it. There simply isn't enough room in the fields of the good tournaments to permit half the deserving guys to play. I think during the daylight saving time period they let 160 or so play. But there are 350 to 400 who want to play every week. Make it read this way. There are 350 to 400 who are eligible to play if they could qualify. There are 10,000 who would like to be playing.

I keep hearing that the answer will someday be in a second tour. I hope this is right. But I don't see that it will help the youngsters too much. I've played in some of those satellite tournaments. They are throwbacks to the old days. The sponsors put up $40,000 to $50,000 but don't draw the names they think they should get for their money. The fans don't come out, and sponsors gripe and fuss to everybody in sight. There's always that newspaperman who writes, "Local sponsors aren't sure they are going to hold this event next year." You start reading that on

Friday while you are playing. I know there are a lot of players who don't want to travel those roads again. Most of us have been up and down that path.

A second tour would be the answer, okay. But the prize money would have to benefit the player. Remember it costs just about as much to travel to play for $50,000 as it does for $150,000. And really, there are enough players for three tours.

I think that if it were announced that the Tournament Players Division of the PGA was promoting two full tours next year—one for the top 100 players on tour and the other for the rest of the players—then there would be qualifying for that second tour and there would be griping from the players who missed the tournament all over again. They would say, "Why can't there be another tour for us. We're eligible to play professional golf. But there isn't a place to play." This is a vicious circle. It would begin all over again.

Now it is not all bad out there. There are years when the tour is really glamorous. But for how many people? Years ago if you didn't make the top ten in money winnings, you were struggling. Now, I guess the top sixty players, those who do not have to qualify each week, are having a ball. But you can bet that their ball can end suddenly. Right behind them are those young kids, ready to jump up in that select circle and send those borderline heroes tumbling back into the graveyard.

I'm a father and I feel I could prepare my son for about anything. But I don't honestly think I could explain to him what he has to face in order to gain a high place as a professional golfer. I couldn't explain the disappointments he would endure. The loneliness he would know. The frustrations seem to multiply as you move along in that business.

But, for twenty-five years now, there have been two sides of the coin as I saw it spin. On Sunday, around the presentation table, you can hear a group of them say, "Boy, this golf is the greatest thing I've ever seen. I wouldn't swap it for anything in the world."

Try a Monday after the boys have qualified and those who missed are hanging around the scoreboard. "I put the best licks I know how to put on that thing out there today and I'm two shots off. This racket here is too tough for me." You'll find more headshaking around the scoreboard than you will find handshaking around the presentation table. The current on tour is swift and deep.

Are most tournaments won by the champion—or were they lost by some poor guy we never hear much about?

I really think that in most cases golf tournaments are lost by one or two guys rather than won by the man who ends up with the money. Of course there are the cases when a fellow comes to an event and runs wire-to-wire with it. But check the records, not many tour events are won by a player who leads every round. There are so many things involved out there that it is just about impossible for a player to lead all the way. You have to consider pairing, choking, hot putters, concentration, galleries, and so many other things. I know this, I've blown them.

The one I remember most is Virginia Beach in 1954. The newspapers never should have said Pete Cooper won that tournament. It should have read, "Tommy Bolt blew the tournament." I came to the eighteenth hole, a par three, leading by a stroke. Pete was the only man who could even tie me. The pin was back in the left-hand corner. I have never shot away from a pin in my life, not intentionally, that is. Oh, I have hit shots that didn't go near the flag, but you can bet I thought I was aiming at it.

Anyway, at Virginia Beach, I drew back and hammered that iron right at the flag. It was a fairly good shot, but it hooked a bit, hit right on top of a bank, and rolled down into the water. I hit another and made a double bogey five. Pete popped his little iron shot in the middle of the green, two-putted, and I was the loser.

You talk about somebody hot? I was warm. I went right to my car. They say rocks fell for thirty minutes after I pulled that Lincoln out of the driveway. I told those officials to bring my check to the next stop. I'd get it there. They asked, "Aren't you going to stay for the presentation?"

"Presentation?" I told them. "If they promise to present me a punch in the mouth, I'll stay. Nobody wants to see a guy who finished second." I was fifteen miles down the road before I pulled off my golf shoes.

I waded through those newspapermen like a fullback going for a touchdown. I told them to write anything they wanted to write. What could I have told them? I had just put the first-prize check in ten feet of water and they were crawling over me for some quotes. They couldn't have printed what I had to say.

I remember when I beat Snead in the PGA at Meadowbrook. He went flying to his car. He had some porter or somebody clean out his locker and bring the stuff to his car. He waited in the parking lot. All those writers were running around asking me where Snead was. I told them, "Try White Sulphur Springs, West Virginia."

It is the hardest thing in the world to sit around and answer a bunch of questions after you have given away a golf tournament or a golf match. I never tried to do it, simply because I knew that some of the answers I might give at a moment like that just might not be the answers I would give if I had time to cool off. It doesn't take me all that long to cool down. But I promise you, there were times when I was better off being left alone.

One year they had bad weather in St. Petersburg, and the Pasadena Golf Club course was wet. It even rained the day we played. They hadn't been able to cut the greens. But it didn't bother most of the guys. They were hanging up 64s, 65s and all kinds of low numbers. I marched off that eighteenth green with 72, a terrible score.

A young guy rushed up to me with a microphone and before I could draw my breath he said, "Ladies and gentlemen, here we have Tommy Bolt, former National Open champion. Tommy, what'd you think of the course today?"

Well, I didn't take time to ask if the broadcast was taped or live, I went at it. What I gave him was rated X, adult audiences only. He stayed right with me, left that microphone planted right under my nose. I assumed when I finished that it was taped or he certainly would have snatched that dude away the moment I started. One thing about that guy, he sure was trained for his work. After I had run the vulgars at him pretty good, he smiled, thanked me, and spoke into the mike, "Folks, you have just heard from Tommy Bolt, former National Open champion and a contestant in this year's St. Petersburg Open Championship."

A real dedicated young man.

Funny thing about that tournament in 1954 at Virginia Beach. It was Pete Cooper who picked up the prize after I had made the mess. Well, in October of 1970, just last year, I decided to play in the Florida PGA Championship at Naples, Florida. I'm leading the tournament with two holes to play. I hit the ball on the seventeenth green, thirty-five feet from the cup. I three-putt the damned thing. Then I par the eighteenth hole and who do you think is right there with me? Tied!

Pete Cooper.

We go three extra holes, I miss a 2½-foot putt on the third hole and Pete wins again.

When's this guy going to start splitting with me? People who study golf might think we have something going. And if they knew that in the old days, when the tour used to stop in Jacksonville, I would be Pete's house guest, they really would think something was up.

Boy, I remember those days. Matty Cooper really put some of that soul food on us . . . . black-eyed peas, ham, greens, corn bread, the works. Maybe, subconsciously, I'm just paying Pete for all those good meals I used to have at his house.

During a round of golf, amateurs maintain a constant conversation. What do pros have to say?

Very little and they are doggone careful with that.

Hogan, of course, never got in trouble talking too much on a golf course. He said, "You're away," and let it go at that.

I know amateurs are constantly exchanging compliments on a golf course. They must say "Nice shot" twenty-five times each during an eighteen-hole match. Golf professionals, when they are playing for that cash, don't do that.

There have been cases out there when a player would take offense at another player saying "Knock it in" on the putting green. Few if any of the pros want the man they are paired with to hole the putt anyhow. I don't know what makes them keep encouraging him. In their hearts they'd rather see him lip that putt out of the hole than knock it in, but they'll look him in the eye and say, "Knock it in." But you can check it, they usually say it after they've holed one from somewhere over there that they had no idea they would make. Sometimes just a simple comment like that can break a fellow's concentration. The best idea is to say nothing.

If I know a guy real well and it is the final day of the tournament, I'll tell him to "Play hard and let's get us some get-out-of-town money." Not only am I telling him this, but I am also reminding myself to bear down.

They tell a good one on Doug Ford. Once he was paired with another touring pro and a home professional for the final round of a tournament. At the first tee, the home pro and the other player shook hands and wished each other well. Ford stayed off to the side by himself during this well-wishing session. Finally, after all three had hit, the home pro patted Doug on the seat of the pants, friendly-like, and said, "Good luck, Doug." Without missing a stride, Ford reached around, patted himself on the hip and repeated, "Good luck, Doug." Sure, it left the home pro standing there open-mouthed, but you couldn't be too harsh on

Ford He wished the man he was pulling for the luck. He was honest about it.

I have little to say to the other players out there. Little good to say, that is. I've learned that lesson. I've stood to one side of the fairway and watched a player hit his shot. As the ball soared toward the stick, I've said, "Nice shot." Next thing I know it fell short into a bunker. He'd look at me as if I was crazy or trying to con him. The best thing for us to say is exactly what Hogan says, nothing.

Put it this way. A touring professional knows when he has hit a good shot. If it is to a green, the length of the birdie putt will be evidence enough. They don't need any cheerleading from me. This idea of saying "Nice shot" sounds friendly enough, but many times it can lead to other things. With amateurs it doesn't matter, I guess; they seemed destined to do it the rest of their lives. But I've hit shots, bad shots, I mean, to greens, and some player would say "Nice shot" and I would catch myself about to dispute him. I would actually catch myself about to argue with him over the soundness of the swing I had just made. Sure, my ball was on the green okay, but I had made a fluky swing and sheer luck put the ball on the putting surface, not good golf.

Back some years ago, Althea Gibson was breaking in on the women's tour. There were some places where Althea wasn't going to be allowed to play because she was black. I remember well that the tournament director for the St. Petersburg Women's Open took it upon himself to see that Althea would play there despite some opposition.

Althea came to town, played her practice rounds, and never let on that there was any pressure on her at all. She is that kind of person. She was a winner at tennis, overcame all the odds, and was out to prove she could do the same at golf.

When time came for the Women's Open to begin and for Althea to start her first round, there was a huge gallery around the first tee. No one knew exactly what would happen, but all the officials were there in case there was trouble. The tension was high. But everything went smoothly. The first two ladies hit their shots and then Althea's time came. She was properly introduced and received a courteous hand from the fans. So relieved was one of the officials that everything had gone well that the minute Althea swung her driver he jumped up and bellowed, "Nice shot." The ball veered sharply to the right, over some tall trees into an adjoining fairway. It wasn't a nice shot at all.

All too often you can mean well by congratulating a fellow player, but it is not the thing to do. And golf professionals are not too free with their conversation. What a game they would have if they treated each other with the same casualness one of my amateur friends treats me. Whenever I play with him, he listens for the shot, hears it, and says, "Nice shot, Tom, where'd it go?"

Can watching bad players swing be harmful to the golf professional?

It works both ways.

There have been times when I was swinging poorly, gotten paired with someone like Sam Snead, and pulled right out of it. Snead has always maintained a wonderful tempo. When you are playing with him it can sometimes rub off. I have had it happen to me.

And it can work the other way. I don't think it is good for a touring player to take time off and play with too many bad-swinging amateurs. He probably shouldn't give too many lessons while he is resting at home either. A certain amount of that monkey-see monkey-do element can actually come into the pro's swing.

I know when I am at home and wish to play a practice round I try to find pretty good players. It would be ideal if a resting professional could find players his equal—but that isn't going to happen. There are many pro-amateur tournaments on tour these days. I know that many times these amateurs feel that maybe their professional should spend a certain amount of time giving them lessons during the day. But that doesn't happen. Actually, the pro may not even be watching the amateur swing. The professional knows what he wants to do with his swing and no one can blame him if he doesn't watch a twelve-handicap doctor out whaling away on his day off. Being sociable during times such as these and not letting the poor swings of your playing partners interfere with your game is sometimes touch-and-go.

Probably if they put it to a vote among all the playing professionals, the pro-amateur tournaments preceding the tour events would cease. They permit them now to help the sponsor raise more money.

Are you sure a guy is safe playing this stuff?

No, not exactly.

They tell the story of the fellow who closed his insurance office one afternoon and headed for a couple hours of fun at the country club. When he arrived, a gang of fellows were on the first tee, jarring the ground with big tee shots. Game was, everybody put up a buck; everybody hit one tee shot; longest ball (in the fairway) got the pot.

Our insurance friend was so excited about the prospects of this newfound wealth that he dropped his buck in the kitty, shed his suit coat, loosened his tie, borrowed a friend's driver, and went to work, street clothes and all.

Whosh! Just a split second after the newcomer had swung, all eyes turned from the flight of the ball to the helpless, howling heap on the ground. News from the hospital an hour later informed awestruck members at the club that their man had suffered two broken ankles. And he had lost his buck because his ball had sliced out of the fairway.

Nothing so drastic as that is likely to happen to the golfer who is properly warmed up for golf. But he certainly should not take full swings in street shoes.

It's been my experience to meet several of my close golfing friends at the neighborhood chiropractor's office. You remember me, Arnie? I had to wait for you to finish with that guy down at Doral last year. Arnold Palmer is a good example here.

Ask them all, ask the privates and the generals in his army why they love him so. They'll tell you, "Arnie is my man because Arnie swings at it like I do. He's up there to hit it over the fence. It's hell-bent for Georgia every time." Where's that army, Arnie, when that chiropractor is bending and crunching those bones?

What I'm trying to get written in the record and what Palmer, Cary Middlecoff, Julius Boros, Ron Cerudo, and a jillion other top-flight players will attest to, golf and back pains go together about as well as golf and heartaches. It takes the rhythmic swing of a Sam Snead to pass through life playing golf and not getting up some morning cussing a back. Snead has had some back trouble, but just a little and just about as much as you would expect a fifty-eight-year-old to have. It can hardly be attributed to his golf swing.

This bit of knowledge should hit home to the amateur. If some of the country's leading pros suffer back trouble due to their golf swings, then the amateur should take heed. Anything worth doing at all is worth doing well and alone, without the weekly interference of a chiropractor. If the amateur can't get it in his head to smooth out his golf swing then for goodness sakes he should get it in his back. He owes it to the three other guys. There's nothing more frustrating to friends than: "Hey, Al, we have to get us a fourth for Saturday, Gus is having back trouble again."

A guy with a pain in the back is a pain in the neck.

Of those fourteen little warriors in that bag,
which is your very best friend?

I'll surprise you here. Most of the big boys will tell you that without a friendly putter, you can call off the round of golf. I feel differently about it. I think that unless a man and his driver are compatible, chances are good that his mind will be so boggled when he reaches the greens he won't be able to knock the ball into a Number Three washtub—and that's the big, old tub they used to use down on the farm.

Actually, I appraise the game this way: driving is 40 percent of golf; iron play is 20 percent; and chipping, blasting from traps around the greens, and putting make up the remaining 40 percent. However, if I had to pinpoint one important part of golf, one thing that I'd rather do well, then it is jab that peg in the ground, put the ball on it, and smack it straight down the middle.

Usually there are a lot of people standing around the first tee. They add pressure to the player. It is a great feeling to know you can walk up there and do to the ball what those people paid to see you do to it—rifle that jessie out there on that short grass. But let's examine it from the ugly side. Suppose you snap-hook it in the woods or push it to the right in trees or, worse, water. First you have to walk through several hundred "oooohhhhs and aaaahhhhs" and "Did you see that?" Bad enough. No one likes to fail miserably at his profession. But then you have to go out there and play the ball. You can't help but let this flaw creep into the remaining part of your game.

Now, looking at it from the other side, golf has to be a happy game. You have to feel good to play it. You have to have a happy outlook to perform well. If you can hit your wood shots straight, everything will fall in place from there on. I have found that being able to drive the ball well can even lead to better putting. Your mind is free to roll that ball toward the hole all the time.

I spend a lot of time practicing with my driver. However, just

117

recently, I spent a lot of time trying to find a driver to practice with. I had an old Kroydon driver. It was seven or eight years old and I'd filled several socks full of prize money with it. About eight months ago, I treated the old boy to a new grip. Well, there's not a leading golf professional in the world who can't take the story from here. That new grip changed the feel of the club. I tried everything with it. Nothing worked. We were total strangers. I went through more than a hundred drivers trying to find one I could use. Finally, in late August, I managed to fix one up. I think I am ready to go again.

No, you can have those guys who think their putter is their best friend. Give me the driver. Don't let it be said that Tommy Bolt is out there running those squirrels from fairway to fairway with his bad tee shots. Let the squirrels stay in the woods. That's where they belong. I'll make my way straight down the middle of those fairways.

Could it be that golf ends once you are on the green?
Seems to me a new game called "putting" begins there?

Absolutely. The game of golf is actually two separate games. One, golf, is a game of propelling the ball through the air in a desired direction and with the desired club for a desired distance. But don't lose sight of the fact that all the things do not always turn out in a desirable manner.

Fifteen or twenty years ago there was far more emphasis on the game of propelling the ball through the air. Players were quite concerned with how they looked swinging at the golf ball. Not so today. Most of the young kids regard the game as simply one of advancing the ball down the fairway, getting it on the putting surface in any manner, and then smacking it in the hole. The motto of the youngster today is, "Gimme a putter. I'll get it in the hole somehow."

But how much fault can you find with this sort of thing? Where do you pay the well-digger? Right at the hole. Where do you pay the funeral director? Right at the hole. Where do you pay the golf professional? Right at the hole. The name of tour golf is "knock it in the hole," and these young kids don't waste time doing anything else. In the late 1940s when you saw a winning golf professional, you saw a sound golf swing, one that took years to perfect. Today some of those super putters on tour look like cavemen out killing lunch off the tees and with their irons—but they are marvels around and on the greens.

Over the years there have been discussions about changing the scoring system of golf. Some people wanted to give points for hitting the fairways and greens in regulation and then the same number of points for putting. This would give the golfer with the good, sound swing the best of it over the player who depended largely on his putting. But that has just been talk. Nothing will ever come of it.

Nothing peeves me more than to be paired with a player who refuses to shoot for the pin. I can never remember playing a round of golf when I shied away from gunning for a flag. But today so many of these youngsters go for the big part of the green whether the flag is there or not. They'd rather gamble on holing that forty-foot putt for their birdie. I guess if anything makes me hotter than seeing them shoot away from the flagstick, it's to see them shoot away from it and then knock that forty-foot putt into the hole for their birdie.

I remember the second round in the 1970 Tallahassee Open. At the ninth hole, the pin was jammed down front, just ten feet behind a sand trap. Billy Maxwell hit his second shot to the middle of the green, thirty-five feet away from that trap. I sent my nine-iron right at the stick. When the dust cleared, Billy was on the green and I was buried to my knees in that trap. I was sick. I looked at little Billy, a guy I really like, and roared, "Say, boy, when did you get afraid to shoot for the stick? These young kids out here have you shooting for the middle of the green too."

Billy wouldn't face me. He was laughing to himself. He knew I was ready to orbit with rage. Even though I was in the trap, I was closer to the pin than he was. He putted first and rolled the ball three feet by the cup. I was fortunate with my blast. The ball cleared the lip and fell softly on the green. It rolled to within an inch or so of the hole. I very nearly made a birdie three. Billy took the longest time lining up his putt. He finally rolled it in for his par. It's a good thing, too. No telling what I would have said to him if he had three-putted.

The format of golf will always consist of two things—flying the white mouse through the air with thirteen clubs made for various distances; and rolling the little darling along the ground in an effort to bury it in eight inches of steel. Until they change, I plan to practice both games.

Are there any golf aids or accessories that you like or dislike?

There have been many I disliked. You never know about them because you do not see my name linked with any. In my twenty-five years as a golf professional, I guess that I have turned down maybe fifty chances to endorse products I felt would not benefit the professional or the amateur. Sometimes people come to you offering all kinds of good cash just to lend your name to a product. But if the product wasn't beneficial in my mind, I always gave them a firm, "Thanks, but no thanks." And there were times when I could have used the money.

I cannot figure out why so many inventors feel that almost anything will sell on the golf market. There have been more than

200 types of putters built and designed, each of the designers claiming that theirs is the answer to knocking the ball into the hole. There have been special tees, special head covers, special shoes, special hats, special any and everything to flood the market, hoping to strike the fancy of the country's fast-growing golfing population. Each of these designers and inventors feels that if he can get a name professional to endorse his product then the public will have to go for it.

Well, I have investigated and tried my share of these items. And I have turned down nearly all of them. Elsewhere in this book you will read that I have always been a person who felt that physical conditioning was the key to a golfer's success. I operate on the theory that my health is my wealth.

You will also read that seven or eight years ago, I met Gil Smith of St. Petersburg, Florida. He had perfected a weighted belt. He came to me with the idea that this belt might be just the thing to help condition the golfer who faced a daily five- or six-mile walk. I never once considered turning Gil down. I tried his belt and it worked miracles for me. I have played many, many rounds of golf wearing the Tone-O-Matic weighted belt. Along with the weighted belt, Gil gave me a set of weighted anklets. I tell you right now that I'm playing golf as well as I have ever played it in my life. And I honestly feel that my physical well-being is the reason. I'm fifty-two years old and I feel like getting out on the course every day of my life. When I'm practicing at home, I wrap those weighted anklets on each leg, put the belt on, and walk the full eighteen holes.

Without hesitation, I will say that I'm in as good or better physical condition than any senior golf player in the world. If I'm going to get an argument, it can't be that my condition hasn't done me any good. I've won all the senior titles I've tried for. I have even held the world senior championship.

Fortunately, Gil Smith did not quit with the weighted belt and anklets. A few years ago he came to me with the Tone-O-Matic Hit-Tru golf aid. This was a stiff-backed, no-fingered glove to be worn on the left hand of right-handed golfers. Now, I'll admit when Gil showed me the first one, I frowned a bit. Gil didn't know why, but I was telling myself, "Here we go again." I looked upon the thing as maybe some gimmick that would not work. But I tried it because Gil was a friend of mine.

I don't think I hit more than half a dozen shots before I was convinced that he had settled on another winner. Anyone who has ever heard me talk golf or seen me instruct or give clinics knows how much I insist on the proper function of the left hand. Well, the golfer immediately gets the idea when he is wearing a well-fitting Hit-Tru golf glove. The stiff backing in the glove makes it imperative that you carry the left hand properly throughout the entire golf swing. Even as grooved as my left wrist is during a golf swing, I noticed that I was hitting better-feeling iron shots with the glove on than I ever could have without it.

I don't care what caliber golfer wears the Hit-Tru golf glove on the practice tee, he won't hit many shots before he realizes that he now knows how the left wrist should react throughout the swing. If he wears it long enough during his practice sessions, he will condition his left wrist to work properly on the course. Each time I go to a tournament I take a couple dozen Hit-Tru gloves with me. I'm not in town two hours before the tour players have taken all of them away from me. At one Florida tournament last spring, I had to borrow one back from a player.

Kermit Zarley had trouble hitting through the ball. I gave him a Hit-Tru and after he worked with it a while he came home a winner in the Canadian Open. Kermit was really won over after that victory. He credited the Hit-Tru glove with the improvement in his swing.

I once gave an amateur player a series of lessons. Never had I seen such fine shots as he would hit when we were on the practice tee. But each time we got together he would have some sad tale to tell about how badly he had played on the course. He told me, "I seem to be able to perform properly while you are standing here with me. But once you leave and it is time for me to take this swing on the course, I'm lost."

The last lesson I gave him was two hours long. I strapped a Hit-Tru glove on him, watched him hit a dozen shots or so and walked off. He stayed there the rest of the time alone. Next time I saw him, he told me that Hit-Tru was the answer. In a very flattering tone, he said, "Now, with my conditioned left wrist, I have Tommy Bolt on the course with me when I'm playing."

There are two big reasons why golf is such a tough game to master. One is that many teachers find it very difficult to get across to each and every pupil just what has to be done during the swing. This is partially the fault of the teacher and partially due to the fact that every individual is different and demands a different teaching approach. Well, the Hit-Tru glove is not faced with the problem of seeking out a different way to tell each pupil. It knows only one way to make the left wrist operate during the swing and that is the proper way. It is just a matter of hitting enough balls while wearing the glove.

The second reason golf is so tough to grasp is that too many times the amateur has played the wrong way for so long that it is virtually impossible for the instructor to break the player's bad habits. The player naturally is swinging poorly and scoring very high or he wouldn't be taking lessons. Here, again, the Hit-Tru glove is a natural for breaking any bad habit acquired with the left hand. You can't swing any way but properly. I feel that for the player who has played many years with an error in the left wrist, it will take much more time with the Hit-Tru than it will for either the beginning or the professional player. For the beginner or professional the Hit-Tru serves as a conditioner or reminder. For the player who is trying to break a bad habit it works as a corrector. In that case, the Hit-Tru must first correct and then condition. It takes more time to do a twofold job.

The left hand has such a demanding role throughout the golf swing. It is the leader of the swing. It determines the accuracy of the player, and golf, besides being a game of power, is an exacting game, a game demanding accuracy. In fact, it was because he could not hit the ball straight that Gil perfected his Hit-Tru glove. He knew he was losing control of his left hand at the top of the swing. He studied his problem and came to the conclusion that he must perfect his own conditioner or reminder. Gil worked a long time with his own personal glove, making sure it worked for him, before he even considered marketing it.

Today, many thousands of these gloves have been sold. Not only have they aided in correcting and conditioning the left hands of thousands of golfers, but they have also aided in firming up the left hands of outstanding amateurs and professionals. I don't particularly have a left-hand problem, but I find that working with the Hit-Tru on the practice tee does wonders toward firming up my left hand. And with a firmer left hand all the way through the golf swing, it is possible to pour that powerful right hand into the swing.

In recent years, after Gil sold his Tone-O-Matic Company to Fabergé, I was retained to do nationwide commercials for the Hit-Tru. I consented without hesitation. I honestly feel that the Hit-Tru glove is the one outstanding teaching aid on the market today. I not only feel that all players should use it, but that teaching professionals should make it a must in their instruction sessions. It immediately gives the pupil the idea of what is expected of the left hand, golf's all-important hand.

Some of the women pros have turned their envious little eyes toward the men's tour. What chance would they have?

Well, let's see.
Some strong-hitting college graduates, men I mean, have tried

and found they have a slim chance. Then there have been thousands of good, local amateurs who tried and found they had no chance. So, where does that leave the women pros, who can't begin to drive the ball as far as even good men amateurs?

I can't imagine where all this started. There's not one phase of professional golf in which a woman professional could even come close to an established male pro. Our best tour putters would beat them. Julius Boros and Sam Snead would beat any and all of them out of sand traps. It would be foolish even to consider they had a chance. Why, they couldn't even play the courses we do. They make their low scores on short golf courses.

Women are always conscious of their weight. I can tell you one thing, put a dozen overweight women pros in competition with men pros, and in four weeks you'll have some slim women pros. They may have a touch of malnutrition, but you can bet they will lose weight. They won't win enough money to buy food.

I wonder who started all this talk, anyway? Could it have been the Women's Liberation Committee? Our rabbits (the young players who must qualify each week for PGA competition) should start a Men's Liberation Committee. Every time the women tee up in one of these Ladies Professional Golf Association events, our young rabbits should go there and picket.

In professional tennis the women stay with the women. They don't want to compete against the men. Have you ever heard of a woman wanting to be a professional prizefighter and challenge men for a world title? I haven't. But I've seen some women who could, maybe, win the world heavyweight championship.

It may sound as if I am being hard on women players. I'm not. The majority of them well know that they couldn't compete with us at our game, on our courses and from our tees. A few of them look at our purses, our television time, and start comparing. Naturally, they would like to be playing for the same money. But it is a fact that the public would rather watch men golfers play.

It would be anything but liberation if we did permit them to compete in our golf championships. It would quickly pass from liberation to desperation. And finally, from desperation to deterioration of what they have going for them at present.

What a racket! Can't you win just one major championship and become a millionaire?

Can't who win just one major championship and become a millionaire? Ask Orville Moody if that's so. As nice a guy and good a golfer as Bobby Nichols is, he couldn't and can't do it. It can't happen to everybody.

In my opinion, and in the opinion of practically all touring professionals, the United States Open is the biggest championship of all. Check the list. How many millionaires do you find? Sure, major championships lead to entrees to huge manufacturers' endorsements, television commercials, exhibitions, and what not. But I'll guarantee you that some fellows could win all four so-called major championships in one month and they wouldn't make as much money as that woman in New Jersey who gave birth to five babies.

After you pick up that prize money at the tournament, you are finished getting paid for golf alone. You have to have something else. What that something else is, I'm not sure. I'm sure it is in some way a gimmick, but no one can pinpoint it. I wish I knew, I would bottle it and sell it in drugstores. In the old days we called it color. Today they slapped some name on it like charisma. It means leadership. It means that whoever owns a full-fledged dose of it, and does something to get his name circulated around the country had better start writing his distant relatives that he isn't passing out any money this year. Because he has just fallen into a sack of it and everybody on earth is going to pester him for a piece of the action.

I don't know who started this idea of a major golf champion-ship being automatically worth $1,000,000 to the owner. They might as well say that ad agencies and manufacturers are willing to pay off on golf ability alone. If that were the case, then Ben Hogan would have gotten all of golf's money years ago. There wouldn't have been any left for anybody.

It's this simple. Ask any of Arnold Palmer's diehard fans what he shot that last round at Cherry Hills in Denver to win the U. S. Open. They probably can't tell you his final score, but they'll tell you he hitched his pants fifty-four times the final nine holes. They'll also tell you he slashed at that little jessie like golf was being played in a fenced-in park and over-the-fence was a hole-in-one. Palmer is popular because he attacks golf. He brings the game down to the level of the weekend player. When that weekend businessman drops out of his society on Saturday morning and pops up on that first tee, he and Palmer are one and the same. He's not going to get the results Arnie does, but Arnie hasn't outdone him one dram. That soldier in Arnie's Army is going at the ball with the same viciousness that Palmer does.

The big extra money for the golf player today—just as it is for any athlete—is in television commercials. Usually, they want an athlete. Since golf is played ten months, the hot golfer often comes into consideration. But look what happened to Moody. He won the U. S. Open in June, 1969. That was six months after Joe Namath's startling performance with the Jets against the Bal-timore Colts in the Super Bowl. Now that's enough. For some reason, sportswriters run over Moody, a quiet sort of guy, to get to Namath. But look what else happened to Orville. In the fall, when television commercials are ripest, Tom Seaver led the Mets to just as startling a victory in the World Series. Moody then stood as much chance of parlaying his Open title into $1,000,000 as he did winning the Congressional Medal of Honor for resign-ing from the army.

It's remarkable what this quest for charisma will do to people. I've seen them buy toupees, lose fifty pounds or so, wear all sorts of clothes, shoes, and hats, eat fancy foods and plain foods like peanut butter and jelly, chase women, run from women, act like women, do all kinds of wild things. Yeah, I've even see them throw golf clubs.

It all boils down to one thing. Some of them have it, some haven't and can't do the first thing about it. Right now, back in that pack, there's likely a young kid with charisma. If for one week, next year, during one of the four major championships, he puts it all together and gets home a winner, he'll make $1,000,000. The public will see to that. Then it will start all over again. The same old, untrue story. "All a golfer has to do is win one major championship and it's instant money."

Then we go right back to Orville Moody and that Namath-Seaver sandwich he ran into.

Athletes! You don't consider golf pros athletes, do you?

I most certainly do.

Do you think it doesn't take a physically conditioned man to hike five miles a day, six days a week, up hills, down hills, through all kinds of weather? Then add the stops he makes taking swings. Then add the time he puts on the practice tee. Then add the mental pressures he endures along the way.

There are many comparisons I could make between the golfer and professionals in other fields. But I'll just stick to this one. In ice hockey, football, baseball, and basketball they have preseason training. This is organized, tough, dreaded by many of them. But it is supervised and usually gets the job done.

None of that happens to the golf professional. Besides being his own coach, trainer, and business manager, he is his own player and organizer. And he had better be good at all of it. It is his personal job to see that he is fit for ten months of tour golf. He

128

must stay in top physical condition all year long. If not, he gets cut off the team. He gets cut out by the fellows who did stay in condition.

At fifty-three, the only allowance I get on tour is an occasional chance to play in senior golf tournaments (tournaments for professionals over fifty years of age). But I still figure my best chance at making money is on the PGA tour.

I am nearly six feet tall. I know my best golfing weight is 175 pounds. I've tried it at 180 to 185. It won't work. Those extra seven or eight pounds settle right on my stomach. I feel them when I'm walking around a golf course. They are excess baggage. I don't need them and I don't compete well with them. The two things I simply do not eat are white bread and refined sugar. I'm afraid of them. I think they will kill you as quick as a freight train. I eat a lot of fruit—peaches, apples, bananas, and grapefruit. I also try to stay away from fried foods. Occasionally, I do eat some fried foods, but believe me, the grease is all gone.

About nine years ago, when Gil Smith talked to me about the weighted belt he was perfecting, I was interested because at that time I had a slight waist problem. Well, when Gil got his product—the Tone-O-Matic weighted belt—on the market, I endorsed it. The big reason I did was because it helped me. I believed in it. I wore it during practice rounds, and I soon got my waistline down to thirty-four inches, and that's where it has been ever since. I also used the weighted ankle bands that Gil developed. They helped build my leg muscles. I would play three or four practice rounds with those ankle weights on, and when time came to play in the actual tournaments, I felt as if I was flying around a course. I could have gone thirty-six holes a day.

Take a look at the professional tour these days. How many fat people do you see out there? Few if any. Those fellows are in good physical condition. Billy Casper was heavy once. He lost weight. Jack Nicklaus was heavy. He lost many pounds.

Instead of answering all the questions, let me ask one. How does it feel to ride in an electric cart? I never have used one in my life. I never will. When the day comes I have to ride, I hang the golf clubs up—I'm through. Many times when I'm playing social rounds of golf, someone will rent an electric cart and throw my clubs on it. I walk. They ride and bring me a club when I need it. Well I don't like that either. To me, that's upsetting my mental conditioning. I like golf. I think I know how the game should be played. You play it walking every step of the way. And you play it with a caddie carrying your clubs. It takes an athlete's body to do this all the time. No one will ever convince me golf professionals aren't athletes.

I have made an attempt to train just as hard for what I do as any baseball, football, or basketball player trained for his work. Maybe we don't have to hit thrown balls, hit people, or hit baskets, but, pardner, we have to hit that track a'walking six times a week, and when you reach that iron shot on the eighteenth fairway, you'd better feel just as fresh as you did on the first tee. 'Cause every one of those shots counts one. And every one of them adds up to hundreds of dollars.

A tired golfer could end up a broke golfer.

Is a caddie just something else to throw in a lake,
or is there something called a good caddie?

You can get fined for throwing a golf club, I don't think there's a fine for throwing a caddie.

I know, I've seen some players who from time to time would have loved to have thrown their caddies. When I look in a mirror, I see another player who has felt the same urge.

There was the time on tour when they wouldn't permit you to have the same caddie more than two weeks in a row. There was a feeling that since there were so few real good caddies it gave the players who could afford the good ones too much of an advantage. I never had much to say about this, but I thought it was silly. The caddie can't hit the ball. And if a player were able to derive great benefit from a particular caddie then, believe me, it wouldn't have been long before all the players would have had good caddies all their own. They'd have had a school out there—they would have graduated a dozen or so Phi Beta Kappa caddies a week until everybody had one.

Back in the early 1950s when you could have your own caddie, I had one, Wayne Hagan, an Oklahoma boy like myself. I always gave Wayne a lot of credit for me winning the Los Angeles Open at Riviera in 1952. He knew every blade of grass on that golf course. It got to the point, midway of the third round, that he'd walk by a little clump of bare ground there and he'd say, "They mowed too close here. There used to be seventeen thousand blades of grass there and they've thinned it out to three thousand."

This is a joke of course, but Wayne really was a good caddie. And he took a lot of the strain off me. He'd drive my car from tournament to tournament, take care of my dry cleaning, my clubs, my shoes, and all the little aggravations, leaving me time to concentrate on my golf. I carried him the entire circuit a couple of times. He had a pretty good deal, he'd clear $200 a week whether we played good or bad.

A caddie can be many things out there and all of them aren't good. There's one important thing I insist on. I want to start most of the conversations. I want to ask the questions and I want particular answers. I'm the player. I'm the guy putting up the money and taking down whatever comes back. All my caddies know what to say. I never ask one, "What club is it?" And he'd better never tell me what club he thinks it is. I don't want to know what club some other pro hit from that particular spot. All I ever ask is, "How many yards is it to the green?" And I want the approximate number of yards, not a club.

Suppose I'm looking over a shot and I have narrowed it to a six- or seven-iron. I ask the caddie and he says, "I think it is a five-iron." There you have three club choices flashing through your mind. You're lost. I've had that happen to me a hundred times. I start fuming. That's when the fans come a-running my way. They see this nice peaceful man standing out there with this young boy, and suddenly the man is ranting and raving and stomping his feet. They don't know what has happened. They don't know I asked the boy, "How many yards is it?" And the boy has said, "It's a five-iron." What kind of answer is that, anyway? It's like asking the boy how old his father is and he says, "I've known him eighteen years."

No one should blame the golf professional for wanting, hunting, and securing a good caddie. Why, there are too many rules in the book which affect a caddie. Therefore he becomes a part of the show. While he can't directly take any strokes off your score, there are times when he can become involved in the game and add strokes to your score.

I never will forget the time I was playing with Leland (Duke) Gibson. Duke had hit a fine tee shot to a par three hole. He putted the ball squarely in the cup. The caddie froze. There he stood, his hand on the pin and the pin in the cup. Instead of making two, Duke had made four! Sure, the caddie felt bad about it. Duke knew that. I knew it. But just the same, Duke was robbed of two strokes. It was a long time before Duke quit chewing on the boy. It got so I was afraid old Duke was going to rupture a blood vessel. He was like most pros, when something like that happens you'd think it was the first two he'd ever made. Or nearly made.

Today's caddie is far too smart for mistakes like that. They've realized their opportunity, the chance to hitch on to an established player, and they have taken advantage of it. They know golf, know the rules, and know what is expected of them. Today, during many practice rounds, I've seen caddies out walking off yardages for their players. That's another load they have taken off the backs of the players. Many of the caddies have their little books out, writing down specific yardages. When the player practices, he asks the caddie how far the pin is from a particular point, and whammo, he has the answer.

I can't vouch for the accuracy of this story, but they tell it on Snead. He was playing the sixteenth hole at Firestone (Akron, Ohio). That's a long par fiver. It was a windy day, and Ole Sambo hadn't hit his second shot very close to the lake in front of the green. He asked the caddie how far it was to the green. The caddie answered, "Monday I caddied for Jay Hebert in a practice round and he hit an eight-iron."

Snead grunted, pulled the eight-iron, swung and groaned. The ball arched high, but wasn't nearly far enough. It came down dead in the middle of the lake.

"You mean to tell me," he fumed at the boy, "that Jay Hebert hit an eight-iron from here, Monday?"

"Yes, he did," answered the boy.

"Where'd he hit it?" asked Snead.

"Oh, Mr. Hebert hit it in the lake, too." answered the caddie.

That's an old one, I know, but it points up clearly what could happen out there if you let the caddie pull the club for you.

Are pro golfers the best-dressed gang of athletes in the world?

We aren't, but we should be.

Years ago, the professionals on tour dressed better than they do today. Some of these kids, and I mean kids making good money, don't care what they wear to the course each day. They wear those wash-and-wear pants, any type of golf shirt, and those horrible sloppy-joe hats. They drape towels over their heads and think only of those twenty-foot putts. Nothing matters but, "How many putts did I hole today and how much money will I make on Sunday?"

Golfers, professional bowlers, and tennis players are the only non-uniformed athletes I can think of. But then in bowling and tennis the dress is about the same.

I have always felt I owed the dollar-spending public a respectable appearance. I have always tried to dress well and look nice for the gallery. I start right down there with the socks and go all the way. The shorts—the white ones with the little red hearts on them—the shoes, the trousers, and the shirts. The hat? No hat, television has nearly all of them playing bare-headed again. Arnie, with that little lock of hair falling down on his forehead, started that. Why, I have as much hair as Palmer does, so I'll go bareheaded, too. Snead? No, you'll never catch Nudie out there bareheaded. But when you see that straw, you don't have to guess who's wearing it, Snead has been under it for a hundred years.

Back in 1957 when I was professional at the Knollwood Country Club in Los Angeles, I really started paying attention to how I looked on the golf course. I hired Sy DeVore, the tailor for the movie actors, to dress me sartorially and undress me financially. I used to go to see Sy wearing my old pants, the pockets bulging with money, and come out with new pants and empty pockets. Back in those days, his trousers were $85 a copy. And I bought many, many copies.

It was really an experience to buy clothes from him. You'd go in for a fitting. Then go back for a second fitting. Then back for a fitting to see if the first two fittings were proper. Then back for a final fitting and final alterations. Then back for the goods. You had some good stuff. The fans who watched you play knew you had the best trousers money could buy. You knew it, and it gave you confidence. Lately, I haven't done business in California. I now have a tailor in El Paso, Texas, who makes all my pants for me. I called them trousers when I was living high with DeVore, now I call them pants—but they are still very well made.

Funny thing has happened to me over the years. As much

134

attention as I have paid to my clothes, it has gone unnoticed by the press. Not by the fans, mind you, but by the press. Even Uncle Sam knows me as a meticulous dresser. Internal Revenue permits me double allowance each year for my clothes. They know that dressing well is part of my professional image and have been fair in recognizing this.

Everywhere I go, spectators ask, "Where'd you get those pants? Hey, Tommy, do they sell those shirts in the pro shops? Tom, where can I get a pair of shoes like that?" Just last year, Foot Joy made up a pair of white and plaid shoes for me. I designed them. I design most of my shoes. No one knows the number of white and plaid shoes Foot Joy could have sold simply because golfers saw me wearing them. But only a few pairs were ever made and sold because the company found that the plaid material stretched out of shape. If ever you see the black Foot Joys with the silver or gold trim you know that Ole Tom designed them. I ordered those back in the days after I won the National Open in 1958. I wore them to South Africa for my exhibitions with Gary Player. Naturally, with those beautiful black shoes I had to wear black outfits, didn't I?

Well, what color do you associate with Player today? Black. Wonder where Gary was when he first became impressed with how a golfer looks wearing black? I'll tell you where. Right out there on the course with Tommy Bolt when he was trying to win those exhibition matches. He didn't win more than one of them, but he found something better. He found a gimmick (wearing black) which he parlayed into world renown. I'll bet that every time Gary reads that he is the Black Panther, he recalls those exhibition matches we had in his country.

But even Gary with his black attire doesn't get nearly the publicity for dressing that Doug Sanders does. To me, Sanders is not a good dresser. He is a loud dresser, not a good one. I don't think Doug has the body that looks good in clothes. He has no shape. His shoulders and hips are the same width. I tell Doug

135

that I have had caddies that looked better in clothes than he does. As for the kind of clothes he wears, I wouldn't go hunting in them.

Other than the fact that I like to look nice, I don't know what it is with me and clothes. Maybe it was because we were poor when I was young and I wore the kind of clothes they sold in secondhand stores and that were handed down to me. But ever since I could afford the best, I put the best on my back. Again I say it is partly because I feel the touring professional owes it to the ticket buyer, but it's something more than that.

I know that when it rains during a round of golf, I don't think about the clubs getting wet, the ball plugging in the fairway, or keeping my hands dry. I think of my pants getting wet and the crease coming out. Why? Don't ask me. But I cannot play golf with the crease out of my pants. There have been times in my career that I could have saved a stroke or two playing a ball out of water. But I wouldn't do it for the lone reason that I would have splashed my pants and ruined the crease.

You'd think I would take a lot of kidding from my wife, Mary Lou, about this meticulousness. Not at all. She doesn't say a word, because in the long run it takes a load off her. Whenever I prepare to go to a golf tournament, she doesn't have a thing to do but drive me to the airport. A lot of guys let their wives pack for them, not Tommy.

Let's go back to last October when I was preparing to go to Las Vegas for the United States National Senior Professional Championship. I left on Monday. I was to return to Sarasota on Sunday. That would give me six days and nights in Vegas. Okay, first I pack six pairs of shoes. A different pair for each day. You just move your golf clubs over and stuff the shoes down in the bag. They are packed. Few people can lift the bag, but it is packed nevertheless. Then I pack ten or twelve golfing shirts, a dozen slacks, two suits, four sports coats, two to four dress shirts, four to six pairs of street shoes, then the socks, shorts and such. Why? Why for just six days away from home does a guy want all this? I want it because I never know how I'll feel when I wake up in the morning. I want to duplicate away from home what I have at home. I want a selection each day, a large variety to select from. I'm never happy when I arrive in a tournament town until I have unpacked and hung up all my clothes.

Back in the days before television when all the players were wearing hats, I had trouble picking one out. I didn't know which way to go. I didn't want one of those little white caps like Hogan wore. I don't think they should have ever made but one of those. On Ben it looked great. It was Ben. He wouldn't have looked the same without that little white thing pulled down over his eyes. But it doesn't do a thing for Gardner Dickinson, Jim Colbert, Fred Wampler, or Marty Fleckman. Nothing but identify them with Hogan and maybe that helps their golf.

They certainly weren't going to stick one of those visors on my head. You remember, the one like Cary Middlecoff and Jack Burke, the curlylocks boys, used to wear. They wanted something over their eyes, but they didn't want to hide those curls. So they went for the tennis-type visor. I'll bet when he was going good back in the mid-50s Middlecoff was responsible for selling 10,000,000 of those things.

Every time I think of one of those long-billed baseball-type golf hats, I can see Gene Littler under it. Either Littler or Doug Ford. Both of them wore the first ones I remember real well. But the thing I dislike about those hats is that everybody who puts one on looks like Littler or Ford. They don't swing like them, mind you, just look like them. I think all golfers look alike with those caps on.

And I knew they weren't going to get one of those straws on me like Snead wears. I'm the only guy in the world to pull Sam's hat off while he was on television (he nearly had a heart attack chasing me). Why then would I want to stuff one on my head?

So, I was left with two possibilities. Either wear one of those sloppy-joe things that Bob Murphy wears (and boy, are they awful) or find me something different. Well, the sloppy joes were out. I even saw Julius Boros wearing one of those things. I couldn't believe it. I was at home; he was playing the final three holes of a big tournament on television. That hat jammed down over his eyes was awful. Here's a guy with all the hair in the world. Hair anybody would be proud of and he's swapped his baseball-type hat for that thing he was wearing. Someone told me they saw Jack Nicklaus wearing a sloppy-joe hat on television. I asked them how many times did he wear it? They said just a couple. I told them Jack was advised to take it off. He has an image to build and that hat wasn't going to help.

When I settled on a hat, it was a derby type, narrow-brimmed, colorful, bright-banded. I had some with feathers in them and little designs on the bands. They weren't conspicuous. They merely kept the heat off my head and were colorful enough to blend in with the color scheme of the day. I had plenty of them, mind you.

But, as I said, television has them all playing bareheaded again. All but Snead. I'll be honest about it. I don't want anything on my head when they are pointing those TV cameras at me.

What about the fan, the guy who pays the freight, can he become bothersome?

No one knows more than I do how much golf needs the fan. No one appreciates fans watching him play the game more than I do. That time I shot 60 in the Insurance City Open at Hartford, Connecticut, I had a big, happy gang of them on those final holes. I was sick when the round ended. I was going so good, I wanted another eighteen holes lying ahead of me. I wanted to make them some more birdies. We had a good time that day.

I recall that as we were coming up the eighteenth, Cary

Middlecoff was going down the first hole. One of the members of my gallery walked over to Cary, and said, "Bolt is eleven under."

Cary, trying to concentrate on his second shot, said, "He's what?" I'll never forget that day and that gallery.

Still, as much as all the professionals know that golf needs the big galleries, there are times when players wish they were out there alone—and I mean they wish the people had stayed home.

I honestly didn't think I would ever see the day when the galleries would be regimented and named. Twenty-five years ago no one could have convinced me that there would ever be an "Arnie's Army" or "Jack's Pack" or "Lee's Fleas" or any of that stuff. Why, these people who bounce along behind Palmer, Nicklaus, and Trevino are nothing. They can never match those thousands of fans who used to follow Sam Snead. They weren't named back in Sam's day, but for fifteen years Snead had the most diehard fans you've ever seen. Too bad some sportswriter didn't tab them, "Nude Nob's Navy." That's one that Fred Corcoran, Snead's Mark McCormack, missed.

It wasn't enough to these people that Ole Sambo was the best of the going golfers of the day. They had to see to it he was. They had to help him out. In 1956, at Miami Springs, Snead and I tied for the championship. We were to play a sudden death playoff. We flipped and Sam won and chose to hit first. His drive soared off the right. It went behind a row of eucalyptus trees. That was trash. That was deadsville. A bogey from there would have put him in the hall of fame. It was so bad that he turned on the tee, shook my hand, and said, "Tom, you win. I give it to you."

Suddenly, a group of people on the tee begged him to play. They did more than beg. They nearly made him play. I hit to the left of the fairway. When we got down there, Sam's ball was in the fairway. It was unbelievable. Someone threw or kicked the ball out there. It was a terrible thing. You couldn't walk through the underbrush where he'd hit the ball. But there it was in the fairway. He parred the hole and won the tournament.

They heard plenty from me. Everybody there knew what had happened. Snead knew it. The late Ray O'Brien was the tournament supervisor. He knew it. All the spectators knew it. But no one did one thing but cheer Snead for making the par.

I don't know how I got in such a good mood by the time they held the presentation, but that was the time I removed Nudie's hat for the TV cameras. He chased me all over the golf course. He didn't want that hat to fly off. I don't know why he always wore that thing over all that skin, but he did. I have even caught him in restaurants with it on.

But all Snead's fans weren't in Miami. He had some in Greensboro, North Carolina, a tournament he won eight times, who had arms stronger than some of the major-league pitchers. Jimmy Demaret, one of golf's all-time fair-shooters, took as much of that nonsense as he could one year, and at the presentation he read the riot act to the fans for assisting Snead in his par making. Demaret tried to explain to the fans that Snead was a great player, he didn't need help. He told them that the rest of the players in the tournament deserved a better break than the people in Greensboro were willing to give them. Jimmy also told them that they had seen the last of him. He was a very popular man there, but he did not go back.

There was an instance at a long par-three hole in Greensboro when a big, fat man, wearing an overcoat, raced twenty yards to the right of a green to catch one of Sam's screaming one-irons right in the chest to keep the ball from going into honeysuckle vines. When Sam hit the low, zooming shot, you could have hung a month's wash on it. It was really spanked and was a cinch to be too far. The fat boy, his hands in his overcoat pockets, spread his coat and tried to catch the ball with the coat. But his aim was bad and the ball hit him squarely in the chest. It bounced back to the edge of the green. Sam got his par. The man got no thanks from Nudie, but he had a sore chest the next day. I always wondered how much he had bet?

Snead was at his best in Greensboro back before they roped the galleries far enough away from play so that a player had to really miss a shot to get it to the people. I can't be sure, but I believe if it were checked that Sam hasn't won there since they roped away the Nude Nob's Navy.

Palmer found a friend one day. This happened at Upper Montclair. Nicklaus, Palmer, and I were playing the final hole there three or four years ago. Arnold and I blocked out second shots to the green and our balls both were over behind some bushes in the rough. When we got there what do you think happened? My ball was over where I'd hit it. Palmer was in the fairway. He pitched up on the green, holed one of those caged snakes of his for a birdie. I complained bitterly about it to the PGA officials. I complained to everybody. You know what happened? Someone asked someone else, "What's that nut griping about now?" I quit complaining. What's the use? I'm the guy who wants the game played correctly and I'm the nut.

Among some of the anxious moments I had during those days at Tulsa in 1958, when I won the National Open, was the time I drove the ball right down a man's shirt. He was one of those television golf fans who did not know what was going to happen to him. Fans later told me he was scared to death before I got to the ball. He kept asking people, "Does he have to play this thing? Will he hit it out of my shirt? Will I have to stand or lie down for him to hit it?"

When I got to the ball, I simply asked him to be calm until a member of the rules committee arrived. When that happened I was permitted to drop the ball. I have often joked about this incident. I have told friends that I wish I had kidded the fellow a bit. I should have told him, "Yeah, hold still. I'm going to clip it out of there with this three-iron."

Years ago, fans used to walk anywhere they wanted to on a golf course. There weren't as many as there are today, and the ones who came to watch the tournaments were ardent golf fans. Today, 50 percent of the people who come out to watch golf tournaments don't know which end of the caddie to hold. If you think I'm kidding you, you get Bob Hope and/or Jackie Gleason to play in the Wednesday pro-amateur event before a regulation tournament and you'll have the biggest gallery of the week out there watching Hope and Gleason. The people who come to tournaments today have to be roped out of the way. Many of them would get killed by a ball, or by a player. One way or another, they would die.

Despite being avid golfers and wise to how spectators should react, the fans of years ago did sometimes get in trouble. In a tour event at Columbus, Ohio, in the late 1940s, Skip Alexander was waiting out in the fairway to hit his second shot to the green. Bobby Locke and his gang were playing ahead of Skip. Skip had his mind on what was going on ahead and was figuring out what to hit. When the way was clear, he never looked behind him, just took a big backswing and cut loose. But he never got to the ball. He never did complete his swing. A spectator, backing down the fairway, had walked right under Skip's swing. Skip had his head caught under his right arm. I've heard Skip tell the story. He is really funny. He says, "I come down with the club and nothing. I looked down and I had me a little man under my arm."

To show you how lucky some people are, this guy was lucky Skip hadn't hit him with his club. He was lucky he backed under Skip's arm just as he reached the top of the backswing. Now, had it been me in Skip's place, the guy would have been lucky if I had hit him with the club. He didn't want me out there with a headlock on him while I was trying to hit an iron shot.

Despite the ropes of today, fans can still get too close to the player. They can be especially bothersome when you've missed a green and have a short-pitch shot. They seem to forget that you have a long club to swing. They don't want to give you room to set up shop. When I have a fairway shot, I want room, plenty of it. And I don't want someone's shadow near my ball. Those shadows are disconcerting because you don't know when the fan who owns that black thing is pulling out of line and heading for the Port-o-let or the hot dog stand. You just can't afford to risk him standing still while you swing.

I always make it a point to turn around and ask the person to back up a bit, move the shadow out of the way. Sometimes this request is enough. They will move. Sometimes no. When they don't I have discovered a foolproof way to get them back. I take the club, reach up and bury it to the hozel in the shadow, and then I say, "If you want to see some golf, then this shadow will have to go." My act is usually followed by a disappearing act.

Still, these are isolated incidents. No golfer on earth loves to have people following him around and pulling for him more than I do. I love to hit golf shots for fans who appreciate good golf shots. Mind if I rephrase that? I love to hit good golf shots for fans who appreciate them.

They used to ask a golf pro, "Hey, man, where'd you caddie?" But today, aren't they asking most of them, "Hey, man, where'd you go to college?"

Get twenty or thirty old-time golf professionals together and yell, "Hey, boy!" They'll all look around. Why, the golf professional who has been around for twenty years or so still lists left or right depending on which shoulder he lugged the bag during his caddie days.

First golf bag I ever saw was at the Lakeside Municipal Golf Club in Shreveport, Louisiana. I was twelve years old and there were a couple of pounds of clubs in that satchel for each year of my life. But I made it around the course. The player tossed me 50 cents for my trouble.

Sam Snead was a caddie in West Virginia. Lloyd Mangrum caddied in Dallas. Hogan and Byron Nelson came out of the very same caddie pen in Fort Worth. They started when they were just eight, ten years old.

You didn't caddie long before you tasted the honey. You got

yourself one club, waded in ponds for golf balls, and challenged other caddies to three-hole games. You couldn't play but three holes and you'd have to find three remote ones on the local golf course. And you'd wait until late afternoon to play. Usually, you'd finish in the dark.

I think the worst thing that ever happened to a good-swinging caddie was the fact that a twenty-four hour period was divided into daylight and night. I recall that I had a dozen youngsters on the run in those late-evening matches and darkness would cancel the matches. About the only competition we'd ever have, other than those head-to-head matches for quarters, would be the annual once-a-year caddie tournaments. No one ever dreamed of junior golf back in those days. The club members would shrug their shoulders once a year, turn their course over to the caddies, and permit one eighteen-hole caddie tournament. If it rained, we played. There was no chance of us having it rescheduled another day.

A couple of things happened to me during those caddie years. One, and luckily, I developed a reasonably good golf swing. I can't remember what I shot the first time I played a full eighteen-hole round. It was a bunch. But it wasn't long before I was cutting the score down close to par. The challenge of the game trapped me early.

The second thing that happened to me back in those early days wasn't so lucky. Apparently, one day at the Lakeside course, someone saw a fellow standing at the edge of a green smashing clubs against a tree. He was co-owner of ten imported, Scottish-made George Nicol irons. But he was chopping at that tree as if the tree itself was alive and dead set on eating him. Whoever saw J. B. Bolt ravaging this wonderful set of irons must have gone into the pro shop and said, "Boy, that Tommy Bolt has a temper. He just made toothpicks out of ten hickories faster than President Hoover can pluck chickens for those pots he keeps talking about."

Friends, that was J. B. Bolt, my brother. He looked a little like

144

me. He and I had caddied an entire week for $15. We bought those clubs together. "How wonderful this is," we had told ourselves earlier in the day. "Here we finally have a golf club for every shot."

On a little par-three hole, J. B. had missed the green. When he failed to get his chip shot on the putting surface, he exploded. Then the clubs exploded. One by one, he snatched them out of the bag and smashed them against that tree. I just stood there. Maybe a tear or two welled in my eyes. But I didn't say a thing. I knew I had lost my clubs; I didn't want a punch in the nose as a reminder.

Now as I think back on it, the punch in the nose wouldn't have been so bad. At least then people would have known that "the little guy with the bloody nose was the one trying to stop the big guy from breaking the clubs. The big guy, that's J. B. The bloody one is Tommy." To save my nose, I have gone through life being known as Terrible-Tempered Tommy. And he's still just J. B., a hellofva nice guy. Well, J. B. stands for "Just as Bad" as me.

Looking back on my days in the caddie pens, I don't regret any of them. I was introduced to golf through caddying. It taught me enterprise, self-reliance and ingrained in me a desire to rise, improve myself. I guess the fortunes of caddying sort of steeled us touring pros against the disappointments in later years. Often we'd sit in the caddie pen for hours and hours, maybe whole days, and not get a job. Maybe we needed a quarter or half a dollar to buy something we really wanted. But we wouldn't get the work that day and would have to wait. Later, when we graduated to the tour, those disappointments of not making the thirty-six hole cut didn't torture us too much. We had known heartbreak a hundred times before.

But today, most of the tour players come out with college degrees, ten years of junior and amateur golf experience, and millionaire backers consoling their every three-putt, duck hook, double bogey. You can't even compare the pressure of today with the pressure we knew. We operated on our own cash, and we

145

counted the silver, too. There were times when we weren't too sure of how we were going to make the next town. It wasn't just me, it was nearly all the players on tour.

The nearest throwbacks to us on tour today are some half a dozen fine Negro players. Most of these young men came up through the caddie ranks. Lee Elder caddied. So did Pete Brown, George Johnson, and Charlie Sifford. You won't recognize them by their college degrees, but you will often find their names up close to the top of the money list. Still, you can't honestly compare them to us. Today, a player on tour has to show a solvency before he is allowed to play the tour. This means nearly all tour players have money of their own, or have excellent backing. The days of hope and pray, grope and play have ended. Besides, greedy country clubs, hustling for that electric cart money, have all but killed off the caddie's chances anyway.

Don't misunderstand, I don't have a thing against a college education. My son, Tommy, has one ahead of him. But there is much to be said for a "caddie pen education" too. You learn humility caddying. You wait on the big boys to go first. You learn to struggle with the heavy bags. You learn to say "Yessir" to some fat member cussing you for losing his ball. You learn humility or you learn to live with black eyes. You learn so much humility that, later, the double bogeys become just a bit easier to swallow. One of the highlights of my life was when I jumped that caddie pen fence for the last time.

Why Florida? Why would an Oklahoma native who lived in Texas, Louisiana, and North Carolina and worked in California finally move to Florida?

I've been all around, haven't I?

I came to Florida to stay twelve years ago. I have lived here longer than I have lived any other one place in the world. Before I moved to Florida for good in 1958, I had been here just as a tour player. But I always liked it. I liked going down to Miami, then to St. Petersburg, then Orlando, then Jacksonville, then Pensacola. It was a great segment of the tour for me.

After I won the National Open, I was looking for a quiet place to rest. I felt that the real rat-race of that turkey shoot they hold out there each week was over for me. Besides smacking those golf balls to those greens, I like hunting and fishing. Thus, Florida offered me the three things I liked most. The only thing was, I had to find a place where they offered all of that close to my house.

I found the perfect spot, Crystal River. They had the Plantation Country Club there. It is a fine course from the blue markers. While I was there I shot the course record, 63, twice—I just thought I'd throw that in. But golf isn't all they offered. There is good hunting and the best bass fishing I ever saw. I thought I knew how to bass-fish until I mingled with those natives in Crystal River. They knew as much about bass-fishing as I knew about golf, and there is just about as much to it.

Crystal River is a quiet place. And after the career I had on tour, I needed to quiet down. Instead of throwing all those clubs I allegedly threw, I threw nothing but a line in the creek. I had me a beautiful home there and owned other property. I stayed there six years.

But in 1964, like everybody, I guess, I started thinking of my retirement days. There wasn't the action around Crystal River that there was in other places, so I looked around. I wasn't looking for action like they have in Miami, Jacksonville, or Tampa, mind you. But I was looking for something in which to invest. Something to occupy my spare time.

I heard of this Par Three golf course in Sarasota, looked it over, and bought it. And here I am. I have been here since 1964. And wouldn't you know it, I still am searching for that peace and quiet. I have my home on Siesta Key. That's peaceful enough.

147

Name of the street? Well, the address is: Tommy Bolt, Solitude Lane, Siesta Key, Florida.

Florida is a perfect place for a professional golfer to live. He can practice his game all year long. Look at the big-time players who live here. Nicklaus, Palmer, Julius Boros, Bob Murphy, Bert Yancey, Dan Sikes, Gibby Gilbert, Bruce Devlin, Gardner Dickinson, Bob Toski, and a jillion others. I remember when Hogan used to come to Palm Beach every year to get ready for the Masters. He would play the Seminole Country Club there. He claimed it did wonders for him. And he must have been right.

They have some of the best courses in the world in this state. That Blue Monster at Doral is every bit as good as California's Pebble Beach. And the PGA National where they played the 1971 PGA Championship is one of the best in the country. Around Sarasota I have many good courses to play. I guess I play DeSoto Lakes, the place where they once held the DeSoto Open and some All-Star television matches, more than any. But there are others—Longboat Key, Sara Bay, and Forest Lakes. Then, on occasion, I ride up to St. Petersburg and play the Bardmoor Country Club. This is a twenty-seven-hole golf attraction that is better conditioned than any of the courses on the West Coast. I like to be around an area where they offer a variety of golf courses to play. I think this is essential to keeping the swing in condition.

And, of course, I'm not unlike everybody else who has settled in Florida. I love the sunshine. I have to have hot weather. There is a joke about me and golf. They say, "Don't invite Tommy Bolt to play golf north of the Tampa city limits after November first and until April fifteenth. He just won't leave that sunshine." I'm not that bad. But they tell it on me anyway.

I became a little shocked a couple of years ago when Billy Casper refused to make this Florida swing with the PGA tour. Casper complained about the pesticides used on Florida golf courses. He said he was allergic to them. Now it could have been before Billy found out what his allergies were, but I remember when he wouldn't think of missing a tournament in Florida. And

I remember when he won at Doral. He wasn't allergic to anything but three-putting that year.

It always amazed me how Casper, a Californian, can kick Florida in the teeth because he doesn't like the pesticides and still live out there in all that smog. It is a puzzle to me why he doesn't get the sniffs out there. Nevertheless, I see that he was quick to say he would play in the PGA Championship at Palm Beach Gardens. That is one of the big ones Billy hasn't won. He'll chance the sniffs for that title, I guess.

Florida, whether Casper thinks so or not, is a great place to live. It is good enough for Palmer, good enough for Nicklaus, and it is good enough for Old Dad. I don't have any plans to leave the peace and quiet I've found here.

*Wouldn't that do-or-die round on Sunday be the
most important one of all to the touring professional?*

One thing for sure, if you are going to make a string of bogeys, you'd better be sure that it is "never on Sunday."

Sunday certainly is the payoff day. It's the day when strange things happen out there. Fellows who have been in and out of the war all week seem to wake up and come flying around with mid-60 rounds. These are the cats who never were in the hunt. They just made the Friday cutoff. They're out there loosie-goosie. When Sunday comes, they know that they are going to make a couple hundred bucks if they live. So you see many of these fellows flying everything dead at the stick. Their putts are bold. Many times they start holing the putts and jump from a so-so position back in the field to a golden position in the money list.

Then there is another group of players. To them Sunday is a very important day, but it can't compare with the first two days,

Thursday and Friday. Remember we always have from 144 to 160 players pitching their tents at most tournaments. About half of these players tip their hats and leave after the first two rounds. That leaves seventy or so players to complete the final two rounds and cut up all the cash. More than money goes with making those final two rounds. The field of players who survive the Thursday and Friday play also qualify for the next tournament. Many of those who don't must qualify in a special Monday round for the next tournament. So for those players who aren't automatically qualified to play in each tournament, the pressure rounds are most definitely Thursday and Friday rounds. If they successfully complete those two days and stay in the field for Saturday and Sunday they have two shots at the money. They can also play the next week.

Then we get to the player who completes three rounds well. He is in contention to win the championship. Sunday dawns and he might find himself jumping out of bed a little early. Breakfast may sound good to him, but when they put it in front of him he may not be as hungry as he thought he was. Now this isn't so much nervousness as it is an uncommon desire to get the war going. He is ready to pull his trigger. Ready to jump on that tee, go to work.

In most cases the players who make it through to the Sunday round can expect to play that particular golf course as long as the tournament committee can make it. It has been proven that people like to see something in its entirety. So, naturally, the biggest galleries pour out of the trees on Sunday. They get themselves a circus. They can expect to see sixty or seventy of the world's greatest golfers climbing back tees some of the members didn't even know were on the course. The pin placements are grotesque. Players joke about them being placed by Hitler or Jack the Ripper. Still, there's an old saying on tour, "Set fire to the tees and cover the greens with broken glass, put the pros out there in gasoline-soaked pants and barefooted, and someone will break par."

The fact that the courses are their very toughest on Sunday

and maybe some of those leaders are being a little overcautious with their shots allows some of those "devil-may-care" players back in the pack to zoom home with super rounds and even win the golf tournament. I know it has happened to me. Once Earl Stewart, Jr., shot 65 on the final round of the Insurance City Open (Weathersfield, Connecticut) and picked up six shots on me the final day. We tied. I had to win that one in a playoff I'd rather have avoided.

Sure, Sunday is a special day on tour. For some, I guess it is really the biggest day of all. It is a day when you don't want any bogeys at all if you can help it. Earlier in the week, if you make a couple of bogeys, or a double bogey or two, you console yourself with the number of holes left to play. You keep saying, "I have time to make that up."

Sunday? There's no making up any mistakes. You see those lapses ever so clearly in that check the man hands you. Instead of getting the $3,100 you would have received if you hadn't knocked that ball in the water, you get $1,750 because you did hit one a foot off line.

Of course you may have been able to have dodged that double bogey way back there on Thursday, too. But the Sunday miscue was the latest one and it is freshest in your mind. Personally, however, the more Sundays I play golf each year, the more money I'm going to make. Not too many bad things can happen to a golf professional who tees that jewel up thirty to forty Sundays each year. Bet you have never heard of a tour player striking because they wouldn't give him weekends off, have you?

Do you think golf is fairly covered by the press?

Newspaper coverage is getting better, but it is more because the public has demanded it than because the newspapers know what they are doing.

Golf is a funny game. You have many people in all walks of life playing the game. They know the rules, know the thinking of the golfer, know his trials and tribulations. Then when some non-playing newspaperman is sent out to cover a golf tournament he can't understand what is taking place and it comes out in his stories. He makes a fool of himself in front of a lot of people who play the game and know what is going on.

Golf is a specialty sport. It takes a specialist, one who keeps up with the game, to write about it. I'll give you an example. Today, it would be hard for anyone to refer to me as Terrible-Tempered Tommy Bolt. I have learned to control myself. Age has mellowed me plenty since those days when I used to launch clubs at the slightest provocation. But still, whenever I am around a sports-writer who has not kept up with golf he will ask, "Tommy, when's the last time you threw a club?" He won't even concern himself that I am a former National Open winner or current United States National Senior Champion. He will go back to that same age-old stuff that they wrote about me years and years ago. One thing I know. These sportswriters would never have been good golfers, for they prove they are lax in doing their current homework.

Not long ago I played a pretty good round in a tour tourna-ment. It was good enough to have a group of sportswriters come around after it was over. You can't believe some of the questions they asked me. They were ridiculous.

One of them said, "Tommy, what do you think of Arnold Palmer?" I couldn't imagine what in the world that had to do with the round of golf I had just shot. I simply shrugged and said, "Arnold's okay. He's a nice guy."

Then another one said, "What do you think he has done for golf?" By this time I was looking for a way out of there. They had me lined up like I was Mark McCormack, Palmer's manager. I didn't want to waste my time in there with those questions. But I did take time to ask the fellow right back, "What do you think golf has done for Arnold Palmer?"

I think what the insecure sportswriter wants is to bring up some outlandish question like that and hope the poor guy says something detrimental. Then he figures he has a good story. These writers wanted me to blast Palmer or something. I don't know. But I'll tell you this, I've known Arnold a lot longer than I have those sportswriters, and Arnold knows far more about his business than they do about theirs.

One time when Dow Finsterwald was pro at the Tequesta Country Club in Florida, he played in the Florida Open at Naples. Back in those days, Dow was doing something good for the tournament. He was certainly playing well enough to be on tour. He didn't have to try to win money in a small sectional golf tournament. But he was good enough to show up to help the field. On the final round of the tournament, Dow hooked a ball into the woods. His ball came to rest on some grass cuttings piled near a tree. As the rules permit, he lifted his ball, dropped it, and hit a fine shot just to the edge of the green.

Next day, he read in the paper: "On the seventeenth hole, Dow Finsterwald hit his tee shot into the woods. He didn't like his lie, moved his ball so that he could get a clear shot through the limbs, and put his second shot on the green."

Now how do you explain a thing like that? How in the world can something like that get in print? This tournament was evidently covered by someone who knew nothing about the sport.

It's getting so these days that you can't pick up a paper without reading that so-and-so is favored in the upcoming tournament. This is ridiculous. No one is favored to win a tour tournament in this country. A fellow who writes that there is a favorite is trying to fill up space. Now in England, where they have betting and odds are published on golf tournaments, that's something else. There can be favorites. But not on our tour. Besides there are so many good players out there no one can tell who's going to have the good week. I think Jack Nicklaus has been outspoken on this. He thinks it is ridiculous to try to pick a winner of a particular tournament.

Another thing that is always appearing in papers is the mention of who's not playing in various tournaments. How many times have you seen, "Nicklaus, Palmer, or Gary Player are not playing in this event."

So what? That's giving those guys publicity they don't deserve. How many times have you read that Frank Beard or Gene Littler are not playing? You haven't. This not only peeves me, it also gets to the rest of the guys on tour. They just can't understand why in the world the writer thinks it is so important to list the no-shows when they are Player, Nicklaus, or Palmer and to ignore the other good ones.

How about this one? "Unknown Leading National Open." That is a beauty. I know one thing—if I owned a newspaper and someone wrote that in a story I believe I'd have to let that man find himself another place to roost. I'll promise you there has never been a golfer leading a tournament that I didn't know. What I think when I read something like that is that he is unknown to the sportswriter. And that writer's letting the world know how ignorant he is. This is probably the worst crime newspapers commit and the one they commit most often.

I know it is easy to find fault. What should newspapers do about this? Well, one of the big things is make sure the man they send to cover golf knows the game. Get a man who knows the game. And for goodness sakes, make sure he knows the rules.

A golf-oriented man will seek out better stories than are being written today. He'll seek out some of the real good players during those Monday morning qualifiers and write feature stories about them. He'll dig for good, readable stuff that will help golf and help his paper relate this wonderful sport to its readers.

Lately, Jimmy Clark, a fellow who played with me back fifteen years ago and was a fine tournament golfer, is back out there trying to qualify. I guess Jimmy has won three or four titles in his life. But you don't see any sportswriters seeking him out to do a story on him. And I'll bet Jimmy could tell them some good ones, comparing the old days with the highly commercial game of today.

Sportswriters face something entirely new in covering golf. They are writing for a readership that plays the game. They aren't writing for football and baseball fans. They are writing for players, many of whom know more about the sport than the guy getting paid to write about it. So it would seem to me the writer would have enough personal pride to learn his subject.

Still, I must take time out to thank the sportswriters. They made me a lot of money. It wasn't their intention, but they did it just the same. Back in those days when I was heaving golf clubs right and left (and I wasn't the only one, mind you), they knew that Terrible-Tempered Tommy made good copy. So that's the way it went. Terrible-Tempered Arnie or Terrible-Tempered Billy didn't have the proper alliteration, I guess.

But the fans came around. They wanted to know who that nasty man was who acted so horribly on the golf course. It got so that I was getting all the action on the sports pages. It didn't make any difference who was playing well in the tournament; all I had to do was to toss a golf club and there it was, a big picture and story on the sports pages. I can't say that I never threw a golf club in the heat of the moment. I have. One missed shot and I used to toss the club right now. It was over with. I didn't take my torment back to the motel with me and beat my wife. I left it all out there where the crime was committed. There have been guys worse than Tommy Bolt, however.

But back to the sportswriters. They loved it so much and thought that it was such good copy that the PGA committee figured something had to be done. I can remember that the rule to fine a player $100 was decided on at the Cotton Patch Steak House in San Diego in 1957. Finsterwald was in charge of the meeting and helped pass that rule. And they all know today that it was aimed right at old Tommy who was making hay while the sun was shining.

I know one thing—the day after the rule passed, I went out and threw my putter fifty yards. And I did it after I had holed a fifteen-footer. I did it because it was my rule and I didn't want anybody else in the world to be the first man fined. I wanted that distinction.

This is one thing I owe the sportswriters. And I haven't forgotten them. They made me a personality. Wherever I play today, people know that there's Tommy Bolt. They all know, the old fans and the young ones. They don't remember me for my National Open win, they remember me for my temper. But they do remember me.

Why, I have been paired with some youngster who has maybe won a tournament and socked away $40,000 to $50,000, and a fan will walk up and say, "Hey, Tommy, who's that guy you're playing with?" They never heard of him. And this I owe to the sportswriters. Back then, as today, they weren't exactly correct about me. I just got lucky when they made the mistake.

Now don't tell me the manufacturers put the same balls and clubs on the market that you big-time pros use. Don't professionals get better equipment?

If it is better, it's better because it is free.

Amateurs can walk into a pro shop and get "hold" of the same equipment pros use—but they probably can't get "hold" of it properly. There is one vast difference in the clubs amateurs use and the clubs professionals use. The professional's clubs are suited to him personally. The amateur doesn't know what's best for him. He knows as much about swing weight as he does about the nomenclature of a Polaris missile. Though most professionals have access to a swing weight machine (yes, there are such things for measuring the weight of golf clubs), they usually are their own swing weight machines.

I know I can pick up a driver, or iron, and know what has to be done to it before I can swing it. Why, it would shock most people to know that I swing a driver that weighs the same as the ones some of the women pros are swinging. Well, this isn't because I'm a weakling, it is because even some of the women pros don't realize that they should have a lighter club. Manufacturers may raise their eyebrows when they learn that I feel the clubs they sell in pro shops are too heavy for the average working guy who doesn't get to play golf more than once, twice, three times a week. Most of the drivers you find in pro shops swing D-2, D-3. You could club an oak tree down with that. My driver swings D-0. That sounds light, simply because the average amateur has heard D-2, D-3, D-4 all his life. He's used to it and by getting used to it, he is used to hard work.

I definitely know that we professionals use the same golf equipment that is available to the amateurs. But I also know that when we use it, it is better simply because we use only what fits our particular needs and swings. We know what compression ball is better suited to us. Most amateurs merely buy a trade name. We do personal work on our clubs to make them fit. Most amateurs take what their pro has sold them and head into the wilderness, just hoping they have hit their particular need.

Remember Big George Bayer? He is 6 feet 6 inches, 255 pounds. He had a driver I couldn't lift. It was E-2, or E-4, way up there. I used to look at it and it reminded me of an ax. It reminded me of hard work, not golf. I never said a word to George about it, but I promise you if he had dropped to a lighter driver, he'd have hit the ball just as far or farther. And he'd have gotten better direction.

Golf clubs are supposed to be your friends. You don't approach golf with a single negative thought. And if you have to ask yourself, "Let me see if I can swing this club?" then a negative thought has come into play. The golf club is designed to help you hit the golf ball. The edge the pros have is not the fact that we get better golf clubs, but the fact that we know which ones aid us better in hitting the ball straighter and farther. An amateur who realizes this will not be a pro, but he will be a better amateur.

How important is the pairing to the tournament player?

There are two types of pairings—the one before the tournament begins, and that big one in which you pair yourself with your score. There's little the playing professional can say about either of them. But the officials will permit any player to sit in on the pre-tournament draw if he thinks something is wrong with the system.

The committee puts all eligible players into one of three categories—former tournament winners, money-winners, and rabbits (lesser-knowns or also-rans, take your choice). If you are a former tournament winner then you can be sure that you will be paired with a former winner the first two days.

For a spell out there once I was drawing the same guy every week. I didn't like to play golf with him. I couldn't play too well in his company, and I asked the officials about it. One of them said, "Tom, you are welcome to come sit in on the drawing with us. That's the best we can do. We put them in a box and draw them out. That's the way it is coming up."

Golf is a wonderful game if you have good companionship on the course. I know amateurs find it that way, for they make up their own games each week and they pick whoever they like to play with. Pros can't do that. Sometimes when the golf pro gets paired with a fellow he doesn't care for, it makes work out of golf. And it shouldn't be that way. I have always said, "There's no better game in the world when you are in good company, and no worse game when you are in bad company." I mean that.

I guess there are guys out there who don't want to play with me. I understand that. I can take one look at the pairings when I get to the tournament and tell you how many of my threesome will stick it out two rounds. I know I've been paired with Billy Casper a couple of times and he quit. Once he left us after three holes. Billy has never said that he didn't like to play with me, but I'm beginning to wonder.

Why, if the Pope were a professional golfer he couldn't do well with some of these guys. He wouldn't like everybody he was paired with each week. It would be impossible. What happens is that you try to ignore your company and concentrate on your business.

All the players out there have their favorites. And their favorites far outnumber the fellows they dislike playing with. So, when you see them running for the pairing sheet, they aren't hoping they get one of their favorites as much as they are hoping they haven't been inked in there with one of those few they don't enjoy playing with. At least, this is the way I look at it. Pairing is so important to some of the players that they have actually sat in on the drawing.

Twenty years ago when I first started, you had two categories of players paired for tournaments, and two only. You had the "pluggers," the guys who needed a decent starting time occasionally so that they could play a dry golf course and maybe make a dollar or two. And you had those high-noon guys, the drawing cards, the guys people came to watch. You didn't catch those guys sweeping the dew off the fairways or breaking the ice in the ball washers.

Of the two systems, I think the way they do it today is by far the fairer. But the very fact that it is so fair, the fact that it is so air-tight sometimes causes it to become cruel in a fashion. Take the tournament we played at Westchester last summer. Ben Hogan had entered. Now if a rule could be bent it could be bent for this man who has done so much for the game of golf. Not a chance, Ben's name was dropped in there with those former tournament winners and he had to go at something like 7:27 A.M. For Hogan this meant he had to disrupt his entire life to be ready for such an ungodly starting time. He had to go to bed at 8:30 or 9:00 in the evening so that he could get up at 4:30 A.M. Ben has to soak his left knee a long time before it loosens enough for him to swing a club. All those people at Westchester hadn't seen Hogan play golf. It was just too bad that they had to see him that early. It was worse that they had to see him shoot 78. And it wasn't that bad a round that early in the morning

It is on occasions like this that I think this rule could be bent just a little. If the committee doesn't feel it could do the player a favor, then look at it another way—do the paying public a favor. Let the guys like Hogan, and I didn't mean "guys like him" because there are no other players like him, have a decent starting time. So much for the pairings the first two days of the tournament.

Now, do you want to know the real important ones? They come the final two days. But you can't blame anyone but yourself for these. They pair you according to score. If you go late, you know you are playing well. If you go early, you know you just did make the cut, and, unless you start holing some putts, you aren't going to cause too much alarm at the pay window on Sunday afternoon. Nothing gets a guy started so well on a Sunday morning as to look in the paper and see that he is scheduled to go to work that afternoon at 1:00 P.M. or so. That means he has to work half a day for maybe half a year's pay.

The Professional Golfers' Association of America?
Seems like it is the Professional Golfers' Association
of the World, doesn't it?

I say, Gov'ner, that is well put.
Every time a player in any foreign land finds that he can

160

outshoot all the players in his homeland, he heads for our little game here and most times ends up filling his pockets full of money. Our PGA tour is helping to keep South Africa, England, Australia, New Zealand, and points east, west, north and south green.

Back in the late 1940s, Sam Snead traveled to South Africa for a series of golf matches with Bobby Locke. Locke beat Sambo 17 or 18 straight. Bobby started putting two and two together and came up with four—$400, enough to get him passage for the States. Once here, he put two and one together, two fine golf shots and one short putt, and walked off with seven out of eight golf tournaments.

Now when Locke got here there were American pros who figured he would be that good. They joined him, bet on him in the tournaments. And there were pros who didn't think he would hold up under the pressure applied by Hogan, Snead, Mangrum, and the other excellent American pros. They bet against him and nearly saw "the great Baw-bie" one-putt them into the poorhouse. After Locke came Peter Thomson, then Gary Player, then Bob Charles, then Bruce Crampton, Bruce Devlin, Tony Jacklin, and others, many others.

Don't think this hasn't been noticed and talked about in locker rooms. The American pros grumble plenty whenever one of those "visitors" walks away with a big bundle of money. Why, I remember when Locke was winning every week. The American players were thinking of ways to get him back to South Africa. This was back in the late 1940s. They were thinking of everything, every way to get him back home. This is probably where the first idea arose for space travel. Someone had to suggest that they should shoot Locke back home in a one-man rocketship. He wore out his welcome in a hurry.

Personally, I am friendly with many of the foreign players. I welcome them to our country and our tour. But I think that their participation on the PGA tour should certainly be limited. I don't think they should be entitled to play any and all tournaments.

161

This opinion, I think, is shared by many of the tour players.

But it will never happen. It can't happen because then people will be saying, "Look at those Americans. They are afraid of the South Africans . . . the Australians . . . the British." It isn't one of those cases when we can laugh all the way to the bank. It's a case of grin and bear it, and practice a little harder, a little longer.

How much help to the beginner is golf instruction material in books, magazines, and newspapers?

You better write it simple. And I mean simple. Remember back in the first grade when we had those primers? You know, "Ned in the First Reader?" Well, that's the way a golf book for a rank beginner had better be written.

Giving a guy an instruction book on golf and his first set of clubs at the same time is just about like giving a non-swimmer a book on "How to Swim" and a pair of trunks. I haven't ever heard of a man reading a book on swimming and then jumping in nine feet of water, have you? If he did, he was ten feet tall.

Instruction material is no good at all to the fellow who has never played golf. Now if an amateur has taken lessons, played a little, and his swing has gone wrong he probably could realize some benefit from a book, a magazine article, or even those daily lessons in the newspapers. But then he would have to find something that particularly pertained to him. Something that hit his trouble on the nose and would allow him to work out his own problem.

The only way to learn the game—and this is age-old—is to take lessons from a professional. Take enough lessons so that you are able to practice correctly. You can't possibly retain enough from one, two, or three lessons to properly put all of it to work for you on the practice tee. So many beginners are able to hit good golf shots only as long as the professional is standing on the practice tee with them. But he can't always be there. He can't go onto the course itself with the player. This is what we professionals mean by grooving a swing. It has been called muscle memory and a score of other things. But it is nothing in the world but a helluva lot of practice hitting golf balls.

I'll tell you something that I think is worse than a beginner trying to learn golf from a book. I think those fellows who take lessons from a professional, learn to shoot in the high 80s, and then take it on themselves to teach their wives and kids are robbing their families of a great pleasure they could have if they were allowed to take lessons, too. There have been cases of husband and wife taking lessons at the same time. A series of lessons, I mean, and the wife coming away from the practice tee with a better golf swing than the husband. That has to burn the guy, huh? You might find that twosome in the bowling alley the next week, or on the tennis court, or boxing.

I remember back in 1950, I was going bad on tour and I took a teaching job at a driving range in Durham, North Carolina. For one solid year, I gave lessons from ten in the morning until near midnight. I got $3 per lesson. It was the hardest work I've ever done and that includes those years in Texas when I worked with that hammer as a carpenter. Some of the pupils would come to me with things they had read. We'd be going along pretty well, I'd think I was making a point, and then they would quote something out of a book that had nothing to do with what I was trying to get them to do. I'd try to tell them politely that if they were really serious about beginning this wonderful game from scratch, then the less they knew about the game, the better they would be. And that's the way I feel about it.

Hitting a golf ball is something very difficult to learn by yourself. But after you learn to hit it, playing golf is something no one can teach you. You learn that for yourself.

What are you doing with all your television commercial money?

It's sweet. It's hard, hard work. But it's sweet. I'm glad I could hold on long enough to be included in this television era.

I'll tell you one thing. They said the camera would start spinning at 10:00 A.M. and I didn't miss the tee-off time. They had me working a double-header. They shot two of them in one day. We got there at 10:00 and they waved good-bye to me at 8:00 that night. But we had one of those New York lunches, you know an hour and a half or two hours.

Hell, it took sixty-five or seventy-five takes before they had what they wanted. I didn't have many lines and I got to wondering if maybe I was history's first impossible case. I started asking around and the guys told me that they ran into the same thing with Mickey Mantle and Willie Mays, who also shot Faberge commercials. From what a couple of them said, if the three of us took the same test, I'd win.

The first part of it was easy. They cut me a nice, pretty tee out there in Central Park and I just stood up there and blasted tee shots with the Hit-Tru Golf Aid riding high on that left wrist. They gave me six or seven of those plastic golf balls and I wore those cameramen out with them. I don't like those plastic balls. They hook. You know me, I don't want to hook one even in a commersh.

But, boy, they tied a tight knot around me when time came for the speaking part. I didn't have much to say on either of them, but it had to be just right. The inflection of your voice has to be right. You can't come out with too much of that Oklahoma, Texas, and Louisiana stuff. If they want a hillbilly, they'll get 'em a hillbilly. They wanted a golf pro for these two shots.

You can imagine how much I laugh these days at that cat trying to eat all "thosa-spicy meat balls" in that Alka-Seltzer commercial. Man, I bet he ate him a half a herd of cattle trying

164

to get that thing shot. He must have eaten a ton of those damn meat balls. Much as I love meat balls, they couldn't have strapped that one on me for all the money in the world.

When the commercials are over, there's nothing sweeter for the actor. Hell, yes, actor. You have to join the Guild to shoot those things. I'm a member now. The Guild keeps records of when the things are shown. They see to it you get your money. Every once in a while I'll walk out to that mailbox and one of those checks will be there, and I smile and ask myself, "Wonder how the folks up in North Carolina like Old Tom on television?" Currently, I have four TV commercials going.

Television has done wonders for all athletes in all sports, but it has been especially kind to the golfer. I mean both at the tournaments and as an added potential in the commercial field. Many of the old methods of golf have been changed to meet the demands of television, and I think this is okay. I know that the guys out there would much rather play an eighteen-hole playoff for some of that big prize money than a sudden-death playoff. But it would cost television too much to remain over an extra day for an eighteen-hole playoff.

And don't think that red light hasn't brought the ham out in a bunch of those guys. It has in me. I love it when they have that thing pointed down there at me. I know when it's on and I know I'm going to hit me some golf shots for all those people all over the country. I concentrate harder. I have more ham in me than there is in Porky Pig.

I often wondered what Walter Hagen would have done in golf if they had televised some of those tournaments he played in. He was hamming it up back when there weren't more than five or six hundred fans. What a show he would have put on for millions of viewers. It's no secret Arnold Palmer loves to play before the TV cameras, but Arnie would have been a supporting actor to Hagen.

Someone asked me one time what I thought Palmer would

shoot if he could play eighteen holes in front of the TV cameras and I told them he might just shoot 36, two each hole. Then the guy said, "Well, it seems to me it would bother the player to have those cameras on him."

I said, "Brother, it bothers me when they are not on me."

Mama mia, what a spicy golf swing I have when the red light is glowing.

These Guys May Linger, but They Shall Not Last!

SOME years ago I was playing in Milwaukee with Gene Littler. He was having a miserable day. I hadn't been paired with this fine young star in a long, long time, and I began studying his swing. Yes, it was possible for me to look at someone I really liked, study his swing, and not confuse myself. I can't look at some of them out there without getting myself goofed good. But Littler I can observe.

I remembered what Littler looked like swinging in years gone by. It wasn't nearly the same this day. We left the golf course before I was sure what had gone wrong with him. Suddenly, comparing the swing I had seen in the past with the swing I had seen that particular day, it came to me.

I found Gene, drew him in a corner, and said, "Boy, you have lost your firmness at the top. You are allowing that left hand to drop. You have to stop that now!"

Gene went home. I mean dropped out of sight for a pretty long time. When he returned he was Gene the Machine again. I mean that "sweet thing" was working for him again. I watched him hit some shots after that and they were made in Puresville, USA.

Back in 1955, I was playing in the PGA Match Play Championship. We had gathered at the Meadowbrook Country Club, Northville, Michigan, for that hog killing. I was to play Lew Worsham, a fellow I had known for years on tour. Well, ole Lew had a bad day. He hooked several drives, pulled an iron shot or two, and I beat him. I will never forget it. This was just two months after I had gotten my lifesaving lesson from Hogan. He had pushed my left hand over on the club in that anti-hook position, and I was having me a field day beating those cats.

Worsham was always a nice guy to me. He and I got along pretty well all the way. I walked up to his locker after our round was over and I said, "Lew, I want you to see this." I put my left hand out in front of him. The back of it was pointed dead away from me toward an imaginary hole. It was in a weak position which I will get to later. I continued, "Lew, that is it. Right there is a license against hooking the ball. And, Lew, I will give you my right hand right here. My right hand to the Good Lord that there is no greater feeling on earth than to walk out there on that golf course in front of all those people knowing that you are not going to hook that little white rat unless you want to."

Lew just smiled a little smile. He said nothing. But he knew I was right. He knew I meant what I said.

There is nothing more agonizing to a golf professional than having to spend his life fighting a hooked tee shot or hooked iron shot. Fact is, you can't fight it. If you grip the club so that you can hook the ball with just a simple flick of the left wrist, then you are not a soldier doing battle against the enemy. You have volunteered for the kamikaze corps. That hook might beat some folks some days, but before it is over, it will take you right down with it.

170

I remember Palmer fighting that thing. I remember how he used to start that jessie way out to the right and bring her back in the middle of the fairway. And then when things got hot near the end of a tournament he'd start it just a bit more right. Finally there, he got so he hooked it just a little—when it was hooking just slightly he was so happy he thought he had him a fade going.

When Tony Lema came out of California and started playing the tour he joined up with a field-mouse terror supreme. Boy, he had those squirrels running out of those left woods with white flags a-flyin'. Finally Tony, on his own admission, got so tired of trying to win money from the rough on the left side that he found his own stopper. He tried the grip I am going to give you later.

"It was okay for a while," Tony wrote, shortly before his untimely death in an airplane crash, "but I think I weakened the left hand too much. I did gain a great deal of confidence, though, and was able to go back to my old grip and win."

What actually happened, and not even Tony realized it, was that he never went back to as strong a left hand as he had when he was snapping off those foul balls. He weakened his left hand plenty, but then never really gained full confidence in it. He wasn't one to practice a great deal on his game. By a great deal, I mean like a Hogan or a Bolt. I have punctured me some shag balls in my day. Tony found a happy medium with his left hand. But it took a definite weakening of the left to teach him the proper approach to the game.

I am a great believer in the simplicity of the golf swing once the fears have been eliminated. For nine of my twenty-five professional years I lived with a fear of a hooked drive. For the last fourteen, I have lived some happy, happy years trying to hook the ball. I can do it, mind you. But I know when it is coming. No more will that rifle shot to the left X me out of a hole. They'll never write on my tombstone, "He hooked one too many."

I meant it when I said it to Lew Worsham in the locker room of the Meadowbrook Country Club and I mean it when I tell you,

"There's no greater feeling in the world than to know you can't hook a golf shot." To me the golf swing is simple. People sure make it hard, don't they? But it is a simple thing.

I will endeavor to give you my thoughts on a few things and hope that together with what you have been doing you will come away from this lesson with lower scores. You certainly will if you put into practice what has worked so well for me for all these years. And, for many years to come, I hope.

First, and all-important, I want to talk about your grip. Forget all you have ever read about putting the left hand on the club so that the V formed by the thumb and forefinger will point over your right shoulder. Forget that and forget about being able to take your stance and see two knuckles of the left hand as it holds the golf club.

The V formed by the thumb and forefinger of my left hand points to my chin. Maybe the left side of my chin. I see no knuckles when I stand over the ball. You might just see one or part of one—no more. This is a weak left hand. It permits the left hand to work firmly through the swing. It permits the left hand to do all it is supposed to do and at the same time eliminates any chance of a hooked shot.

Larry Hinson, the fine young man who suffered polio and now has overcome all that to prove himself a winner on the tour, is a perfect example of what I'm trying to say about the left hand. Larry's left arm was so bent by polio that he has to put the left on the club just right. He then is free to pour that powerful right hand of his into every shot without the slightest worry about hooking the ball out of play.

After you have placed the left hand on the club as I directed, then place the right on the club so that the palms of the hands point toward each other. This means that the V formed by the thumb and forefinger of the right hand also points in the direction of the chin. It does not point over the right shoulder as that pro around the corner might have told you or as you might have read in some daily newspaper. Both V's, the left and right, point to the chin.

Your hands are now on the club in a fashion that has revolutionized golf since Ben Hogan worked out this theory in his hospital room back in the late 1940s after his automobile accident. Ben was another who used to have nightmares over hooked tee shots. But he did more than talk about it, he found out how to stop it. And it was Ben who saved my career back in 1955. I went to him and all but got on my knees for help. This is the biggest thing he did for me. Except maybe tell me I was hitting it correctly. When Hogan tells you you are doing it right it is enough mental therapy to last six months.

With your hands on the club in the manner described you must be sure that the major pressure applied to the club is with the last three fingers of the left hand. This is all-important because of the command of the swing which your left hand and arm assume. I am always exercising to strengthen the last three fingers of my left hand. Every time I pick up a golf club, I use just those fingers. You might try this on your clubs. If you cannot pick up your clubs with those fingers then either your grip is bad or you own clubs too heavy for you.

Let's look at my grip now. I have my left hand weak. I see no knuckles, the V is pointing at my chin. I am firm with my last three fingers. Now, I put the right hand on the club. My little finger goes over the knob of the forefinger of my left hand. The only pressure I have on the club with the right hand is in the ring finger and the middle finger. The thumb is on top of the shaft and the forefinger is looped under.

If you have followed this correctly, you will surely see how important it is to have pressure with the last three fingers of the left. That's the most contact you are making with the club itself, isn't it?

I'll go along with the old thought that the golf club is an extension of the left arm But I'd like to add that the hinge they so often refer to at the hand and wrist had better not be considered a hinge at all. You must be firm with the left at the address of the golf shot, at the top of the swing, and all the way down to and through the golf shot. But, wait, we don't rush the shot when we make it—let's don't rush it here.

I have always thought that the word "grip" was a bad one in golf. But, for want of a better one here, I will go along with grip. But I will also tell you that you should know the difference between a friendly attachment to the golf club and a death grip. Your grip, and I refer here to the actual holding of the club, should not be a death grip. Learn to hold the club with the muscles of the hands. The left hand is a combination of finger-palm grip, firm with those back hand muscles, and the right is strictly a finger grip. Now that we have the controls of this big airplane in our hands, let's see if we can climb into the cockpit correctly and get this big, bad bird off the ground.

You know learning to fly is not half as difficult and dangerous as learning to play golf. A man learning to fly is more reasonable. He and his instructor are both practical men. Neither one wants to see a solo flight until the student can take off and land the plane. But golf pupils and golf instructors are different. They, the golfers, will venture out into the wild blue yonder without flight plan, maps, radio, or parachute. Some of them even take off without an airplane. And some of the instructors, who incidentally have never soloed themselves, take money from these "players" and, like the barber, yell, "Next!"

I can't think of a more comfortable position than the correct one over a golf shot. It gripes me to read an instruction article wherein the author simply tells the student, "to take a comfortable stance over the ball." That's like yelling to the non-swimmer in twelve feet of water to flap his arms.

I don't say, "Take a comfortable stance over the ball." I suggest you take, "THE comfortable stance over the ball." Here again, I differ with some of the old-time teachings you have heard. I am not one who believes that you must place your feet the width of

174

your shoulders. I don't do it. Mine are wider than my shoulders. Hogan's feet are wider than his shoulders. Many tournament players place their feet wider than their shoulders. And, some place theirs closer together than the width of their shoulders.

The width of the feet determines the amount of body-turn you will have. If your feet are closer together, you get more body-turn. If wider, less body-turn. I feel that the less body-turn I have, the less margin for error I have at the top of the swing. I would suggest that a player with feet close together, striving for a greater body-turn, would have to concentrate on a slower backswing. The hands then would have to travel farther up and around. If the player were too quick with his takeaway then there is the definite possibility of a breakdown of the left arm, wrist, or hand at the top.

This, my friend, is the one that has put so many of them in the rest home. Hard to believe a fellow could have a mental breakdown simply because he has a breakdown of the left wrist on his backswing, isn't it? And there's little cure for this, because there aren't enough doctors around who swing well enough to diagnose the patient's problem. They'd rather wrap it around his home life, his business, or something with test cases involved.

I find that I'm comfortable with my feet spread two to three inches wider than my shoulders. And I have the shoulders of a carpenter mind you. You certainly could do the same. When you take your stance, know that the weight is evenly distributed on both the right and left feet. BUT that weight definitely should be on the insteps of both feet. I've heard them say that the weight should be back through the heels. The emphasis there is incorrect. My weight is not back through the heels. My weight is concentrated on the insteps. This brings my knees toward each other in knock-kneed fashion. I've read articles that urged the players to assume a knock-kneed position over the ball. That's crazy. It should read that if the player plants his feet, weight to the insteps, the knees then will point toward each other.

Last fall when I was playing in the National Seniors Championship at Las Vegas, Tom Draper, an outstanding senior star from Detroit, an amateur player who once won the North and South, was talking on this subject. Tom was threatening to take the spikes off the instep of both his shoes. I raised my eyebrows when he mentioned this because I knew exactly the direction in which Tom was working to secure a more workable stance over his shot.

If you have ever read anything Hogan wrote about golf or have seen this little man play, then you know that he kicked his right leg just before address. That's what has been written, he kicked his right leg before address. Well, Ben was kicking that right foot. He was kicking it down into the ground. He planted that right foot deep. It was like a strong oak tree when he stood over the ball. Oh, I know that there has been some talk of Ben shoving off into the shot with his right leg. He may have done a little of that. But the important thing to him was getting that strong, comfortable feeling while he was over the shot. He wanted something firm under him when he turned away from the ball.

I imagine that someday a shoe manufacturer will build golf shoes with longer spikes on the outside to enable the golfer to get a better stance. Or they might just eliminate the spikes from the inside. Either one will serve the purpose. It certainly isn't the worst idea anybody ever had. The moment the player stands up over the ball, the shoes he is wearing would automatically drop him into the proper position.

The weight distribution along the inside of the feet is so important to golf. Not only does it pull the knees in, but that flexing of the drawn-in knees causes a protrusion of the back "hip area" (call it what you like), which in turn causes a slight bending at the waist as you reach with arms and club to address the ball.

Once more I'd like to point out to you an error I have read in instruction. Some time ago, in a newspaper or magazine, I read that a professional was insisting that too many players went after the ball "stiff-kneed." He wrote, "Don't do that. Flex the knees

176

for better golf." This guy could very possibly put his already ill patients in the intensive-care ward.

You cannot tell someone to "flex his knees" and let it go at that. The knees flex if the feet are properly placed, an inch or so wider than shoulders, weight on insteps, evenly distributed from toes to heels. You cannot assume golf's proper stance stiff-kneed. If you have faulty knee action it can be traced to the major error, the feet.

There you have MY grip and my stance. And could it be any easier? No.

But here we go.

If there is one question that has been asked more than any other concerning golf instruction, then this is it:

"WHAT'S THE FIRST MOVE GOLF PLAYERS MAKE WHEN THEY START THEIR BACKSWING?"

My answer:

"IF THEY ANSWER ANYTHING BUT 'ALL AT ONCE' THEN THEY MAY BE GOOD PLAYERS BUT THEY HAVE SOME HOMEWORK TO DO."

Yes, there are segment swingers on tour. There are players who start going back with hands first, arms first, hips first, or shoulders first. THESE GUYS MAY LINGER, BUT THEY SHALL NOT LAST.

Skip Alexander is a former touring player who is now settled in Florida. I talked about Skip earlier in the book. Until his accident some twenty years ago, Skip proved he was destined to become a super player on tour. His is one of the truly courageous stories in all of sport. The fact that Skip would have become a great player has been evidenced since by the knowledge he has of the game.

A friend of mine asked Skip one day, "How does Tommy Bolt get that club back in the perfect position every time? He makes it look so easy."

Skip, who has seen me play many times, answered: "He just snatches it up there."

177

I smiled when I heard this. I like that description, maybe because when I'm over a shot, I want my grip and stance to be so perfect that I can give the impression that despite any distraction occurring outside, I'm prepared to "just snatch that club back into the proper hitting position."

This approach is all relative to the proper gripping and holding of the club and the proper foot positioning. If these things are done properly, then where else is there to go but to the right position at the top? (Here, I purposely withhold a little item called tempo. You'll get that later.)

I repeat, everything happens at once when I move into my backswing. And if I did the first two things, gripped and attained my stance correctly, then everything moves properly.

I am going through these motions one at a time, but don't lose sight of the fact that they are operating ALL AT ONCE. My left is in full control of the hands because I was sure I had gripped firmly with those last three fingers. There is full extension of the left arm because I was certain of my grip and I have that comfortable instep balance. There is no need for my predominantly stronger right to take over to regain balance. (You know that if a right-hander stumbles moving in a backward position, he stabilizes himself from the right side, which is bad for golf. That, too, will be covered in the tempo section.)

My shoulders have turned under because of the extension of the left hand and arm. My hips have turned because my weight has shifted ENTIRELY TO THE INSTEP OF THE RIGHT FOOT. There I am. As Skip said, I have snatched her up there. For your benefit, I have swung the club back there all at once.

How far do you go back? I read that some of them teach, "Go back until the club is parallel to the ground." Funny, those instructors could not teach me to hit the ball. And I have fair equipment to start with. If you ask an honest instructor, "How far do I go back with the club?" the only answer he could give you would be, "I don't know." He would be telling you the truth and you would have to pay him his fee. And, be sure, you have a

178

friend there, so stick with the lessons. A good instructor could stick with you, watch you hit shots, and tell you. But this cannot be answered in a classroom.

I cannot get the club back parallel to the ground and still own it. By own it, I mean have control of it with my left hand and arm. The club can only be taken back as far as the body-turn will permit. The moment that left hand has broken up (with wrinkles in back of the hand), broken down (with an upward protrusion of the wrist), or opened the slightest where the little finger is holding, then you know how far you can carry the club back. And it is not to the point where you detected one of the errors. It was somewhere short of this disaster area, at a point where you still had control of the club.

You recall I mentioned finding an error in Gene Littler's swing. It was right here. Gene was forcing the club down to the parallel. This forcing action came after he had lost control with the left hand. He was playing with a scatter gun.

This is truly a trouble area of golf. It is the reason the game is so hard to master. It is the reason that 90 percent of the people who play golf cannot break 90. A bad grip can cause the breakdown of the left at the top. Gripping correctly but holding the club too tightly causes it. Faulty foot positioning can cause it.

AND A BAD TEMPO CAN CAUSE IT.

It would be senseless for me to tell you that the majority of good players on tour have bad grips and do not know how to hold the club correctly. Most of them have fine grips. Most of them hold the club correctly. By the same token, most of them stand to the ball well. Then why don't all of them play well all of the time?

Well, aside from putting (and I'll read YOUR stuff about this hellish game), tempo is the deciding factor in most golf tournaments. I say this assuming all players involved are concentrating on their work properly. But I believe the players not concentrating were lost back there on Friday when they cut the field. Your tempo has as much to do with how far you can carry the club

179

back as anything. Your tempo is your own personal problem. I can stand out there with you and tell you if you are in control of the club. But I can't tell you that you can swing faster and still have control.

The problem is—and it takes practice to solve—how fast can you move into your backswing and not commit any errors with your left hand. Palmer could move awfully quickly, couldn't he? Whew! Ever see his hands and arms? Powerful. Cary Middlecoff moved slowly. Lloyd Mangrum moved slowly. Hogan? Faster than Middlecoff and Mangrum. Slower than Palmer.

But what these players had in common, and I guess I'll throw Arnold in there because he is so physically strong, is that they did not move back at peak speed. They always played at a tempo that left them something to spare.

Put it in miles per hour. Say I could take the club back thirty miles per hour and still control the left hand at the top. Then I would work to take it back twenty-two miles per hour all the time. All the time, that is, until I needed the extra eight miles per hour. This might occur on a long par five. Or it might never occur. At any rate, I would always be playing within myself. Always owning my golf club at the top of the swing.

A faulty tempo not only leads to a breaking down of the left hand. It can lead to pulling the player off the instep of the right foot going back. That can happen before the left gives way. Then you have rolled to the outside of the foot and you cannot possibly get back to the hitting area.

You must work on that tempo for yourself. Strive to find the peak of your tempo. Then fall down under it considerably. Never swing the club as fast as you can. Hold some in reserve. The amateur would be better off never reaching his peak at any time.

I have always thought that tempo was something players could achieve by practicing with long irons. And I mean all players. Golfers don't know enough about physics to understand that a four-iron is manufactured to hit a ball farther than an eight-iron will. I am talking about pros, amateurs, and me. I feel that when a player is standing over a four-iron shot, or any long iron, he is his own worst enemy.

You read where the instructor suggests you make sure you take the club all the way back on long irons. What I think should happen is that you make sure you maintain the same tempo with long-iron shots. There you see you have a lot of yards to cover to the green. The tendency is not to trust the loft of the club to do the work, but to swing harder. There's your tempo. Gone. Any of the many errors caused by swinging too fast can come into play and the accuracy of the iron shot is destroyed. I find that hitting long irons into the wind is the best thing in the world for working on my tempo. Try it.

If you move through your early golfing life with a good tempo, then you will be able to play pretty decent golf all your life. Years ago, I marveled at the tempo of Sam Snead and E. J. (Dutch) Harrison. Today, they are fifty-eight and sixty years old. And they are fine players. I still say Ole Dutch, if he had had the heart and the power to concentrate on his business, would have been the greatest of them all. Somehow Dutch didn't seem to have that killer instinct. And he always was one who loved to gamble. He'd gamble on anything.

It was as recently as 1968, at the PGA Senior Championship, Palm Beach Gardens, Florida, that I trapped Dutch. Snead and I were close to the top going into the last round. Dutch sneaked around and bet $500 on Snead. He was paired with me the final day.

Someone had told me Dutch had bet against me. So I was prepared for any of his tricks on the course. I could see he was going to slow the thing down. So I slowed down and had me a picnic. I shot 67 that last day and won the tournament. When we finished, Dutch's chin was dragging the ground. As we walked off the eighteenth green, I patted Dutch on the rump and said, "Now, Dutch, let that be a lesson to you. You bet against me and lost your money. Don't let Ole Dad catch you out here sucking eggs like this anymore "

I have always liked that Dutch. I think he has been a grand old guy for golf. You couldn't count the people he had done favors for out on that tour. They never hesitated to come to Dutch for favors and he never turned one of them down when he could help.

But this has little to do with instructional golf except that I wanted to point out that Dutch Harrison, despite being sixty years old, is still a winning golf player because he has tremendous tempo. He always played within himself.

Tempo is the measure of how every person who swings at a golf ball will succeed. Tempo is the reason you can put 144 outstanding golf players in one tournament and separate them in seventy-two holes. Unless it is practiced, tempo can come and go daily, hourly, or from shot to shot. This is why you should never play to your maximum tempo. Leave room there for those days when you are a bit fast, but manage to stay within your capabilities.

The tempo of the swing not only controls the distance you take the club back, but if it is proper, it also produces a sensation as if you had paused at the top of the swing. I do not think I pause. I think I take the club back to a point where I have maximum control. I can go back farther, but seldom do. Then, again, ALL AT ONCE, I move into the shot.

I don't start down with hands first, shoulders first, hips first, or by placing my left foot down on the ground first. I go into the shot ALL AT ONCE.

The extended left arm is my guide to and through the golf shot. The grip I explained is protection against the hook. I have no fear whatsoever of the right hand overpowering the shot as long as I know I can continue the extension of the left hand and arm through the ball.

You can pick up instruction pieces that read: "Don't hit from the top with the right hand." Here is another author who couldn't teach me to play. How are you going to hit from the top if you have maintained control with the left going back? If the tempo was such that the left never broke down, your balance was such that you stayed on that right instep, then you are in perfect position to go into the ball with your left leading the way. The right hand will be there. And when it gets there you receive maximum power if your left arm continues its extension through the shot.

I once heard Billy Graham preaching. In talking about faith in the Good Lord, Billy compared it to driving along an expressway. Here is close to what he said, but not word for word.

"If you are traveling down an expressway and come to a high hill, you don't slow your car from fifty-five miles per hour to ten miles per hour so that you can coast to the top of the hill and see for sure if the highway department has completed the road on the other side. You continue along at fifty-five miles per hour with faith in the road department that there is continued construction."

Blushing a bit, I confess that when I heard this, I compared it to the golf swing. To the downswing of a golf club. I can't tell you how many people I've seen swing who do not have faith in what they are doing.

We can go back to an earlier illustration I gave you. Remember when Tony Lema changed his left hand from a strong position over to the left to a weak one on top of the club? Remember when he said he tried it and found he was hitting the ball to the right? He confessed he thought that the new position gave him the confidence that he would never again hook himself in trouble. Tony would never have had to change his new grip if he had had complete confidence in it. He had to know that he would eventually overcome hitting shots to the right when he was confident he could pour his right hand into the shot.

The entire golf swing hinges on the faith the player has in it. He must have full faith in the positions he acquires during the swing and the movements he makes. They should all be with one reason in mind, to move that golf ball in the desired direction and for the desired distance.

I have this faith. I maintain it because I practice it many hours each week. I understand that my job in gripping the club, gaining the balance over the shot, swinging the club back is nothing but a preparation for the final, decisive move. That one down, into, and through the golf ball.

This has to be done with the left hand and arm moving in an extended arc through the entire swing. Check off what happens if that left moves correctly all the way through:

The left shoulder moves up from its position under the chin.

The right shoulder follows in a high to low arc, passing under the chin just after impact.

The hips start an unrushed movement to the left and are nearly square to the ball at impact.

The right elbow is permitted to pass in close to the body, maintaining the automatic cock in the right wrist until that vital moment at the ball.

The weight is moving smoothly from the right foot to the full left foot.

The right foot has left the ground immediately. There is no spinning of the right heel. Many players, losing control of the club with their left hands, can check this by checking their right heels. Place a golf ball by your right heel as you address the shot. If, when you start down with the club, you move this golf ball in the slightest, you have spun off the shot. You are in trouble. You had better check closely on your tempo or your foot positioning at address.

I make an effort to hit against the instep of my left foot. I realize this is impossible to maintain throughout the entire swing. When all my weight rushes to that left foot, the entire foot has to come into play in order to control all that weight. However, this does enable me to achieve a complete extension of my left arm and does give me the firm left side to hit against.

I will admit I have been hard on golf instructors in this article. That's me, I guess I know how I hit the ball. I know how Hogan, Palmer, Nicklaus, and al¹ the great ones hit it. I guess I become angry when I read what some people, who never were able to produce championship golf shots, feel is the proper approach to this grim problem we all face. Few of them concentrate properly on the do's. They seem to make their living teaching golf's don'ts. Golf is a game in which you are trying to do something. Make it that. Don't make it a game in which you are trying not to do something. I told you, I traveled that road for nine years. I tried NOT TO HOOK for nine years. I find it much better trying TO knock her stiff every time I swing at a green.

Here, I would like to put in a plug for all instructors of the game. I would encourage you to hire your home professional to observe you when you are working on stance, tempo, and take-away, and the downswing through the ball. Ask him to watch and see if you are making a complete extension through the ball with your left arm. You shouldn't take too much of his time. When you finally achieve this knack, then the shots you produce will be the envy of the barnyard. You'll know you are doing it correctly.

There is one final question that I am asked so often.

"Okay, Tommy," someone will begin, "if the golf swing is as simple as you say it is, then why do the pros spend so much time practicing?"

I can't answer that for all professionals. But I can for myself. There are two things I work for most. The first and foremost is a firmness with my left hand through the golf swing. The second is my tempo.

First, the firmness. As you read earlier in this book, some years ago the Tone-O-Matic Hit-Tru Golf Aid was introduced to me by Gil Smith of St. Petersburg. I found that this glove was perfect for what I was trying to achieve on the golf course. Heck, I wore the thing playing and I thought maybe Gil had started something that would make par golfers out of everybody. This glove, backed with a stiff though pliable substance, serves as a constant reminder of what the left is supposed to do during the entire swing. If it doesn't work for you, then your swing is incorrect. It is that simple. If you wear this glove and cannot hit a golf shot, then you are going after the game in the wrong way. I can say nothing stronger than that.

But the glove worked for me and it worked for so many other people that I couldn't wait for Gil to get it okayed by the United States Golf Association. That group decides on all items worn or otherwise employed in the playing of amateur tournament golf. The pros, I might add, go along with the recommendations of the USGA.

It never dawned on me that the USGA wouldn't approve it. But they didn't. They classified it as an aid. An aid? What are spikes? What is an ordinary glove? What are glasses to people with poor vision? What is that straw hat to Sam Snead? You don't think Sam could play bareheaded and break 80, do you?

But Gil accepted the USGA's ruling. He's a tough guy. Not even the USGA can push Gil off something good. He went right on making those Hit-Trus and players, realizing how important the firmness of the left hand was to the swing, kept right on buying them. I have continued to push the glove. I feel that even though a player cannot take it into tournament play with him, he most certainly can practice with it whether he is on the practice tee or playing a practice round. I do. I feel that it strengthens my left wrist. It makes it possible for me to grip better and it definitely conditions the firmness I strive for.

Quite simply, the Hit-Tru provides me with the faith in that left hand I need all the way through the swing. With this confidence I am therefore able to maintain a better tempo. This is why I practice my golf so much. These are the things I practice, and that little Hit-Tru is what I practice with.

In closing out this instruction, I would like to request that you do not throw away what you have been playing with all these years. I urge you to compare what has worked so well for me with what you have been doing. Maybe you will find that you are off just a little somewhere along the line.

First, ask yourself what you are trying to do when you play. Are those things positive? Be sure you are trying TO DO something rather than trying NOT TO DO something.

Then check your grip. Check your stance and balance. Take the club away from the ball ALL AT ONCE. Do this with a tempo that provides you control with that left hand and arm all the way. Remember the length of your backswing is determined by how far back and how high you have gone with complete control of the club. Try to stay just below this peak position at all times. Leave yourself a certain ma: gin for error. The downswing, as was the backswing, is ALL AT ONCE.

You hit golf's jackpot when you have mastered the technique of extension of the left arm down, to, and through the golf ball. Have faith. The rest will happen.

Finally, I urge you not to junk everything you have worked on all these years. Just compare what I have said here with what you have been doing.

You might remember this, however. What I told you here won the National Open Championship for me in 1958. I killed every cat in the alley.